WHAT HAS HAPPENED TO BASEBALL?

WHAT HAS HAPPENED TO BASEBALL?

A Concentrated Look at Analytics, Poker, and Intuition

DANIEL ARFIN

Made in Charleston, SC
www.PalmettoPublishingGroup.com

What Has Happened to Baseball?
© 2020 by Daniel Arfin

All rights reserved. This book or any portion thereof may not be reproduced or used in any manner whatsoever without the express written permission of the publisher except for the use of brief quotations in a book review.

ISBN-13: 9781641117708
ISBN-10: 1641117702

CONTENTS

Introduction	1
1st Inning: The Manager versus the Head Coach	6
2nd Inning: Who Should Bat Second? And Where Should the Pitcher Hit?	10
3rd Inning: The Starting Pitcher Is Dominating, but We're Still Going to the Bullpen	28
4th Inning: Strikeouts, Home Runs, and Walks	51
5th Inning: Proposed Changes	65
6th Inning: Hot, Cold, Clutch, and Choking	94
7th Inning Stretch: The Shift	118
8th Inning: When Did Professionalism Become Unimportant?	120
9th Inning: What Has Happened to Baseball?	132

INTRODUCTION

I'm a distraught thirty-four-year-old baseball fan.

I'm a distraught Mets fan, too, but that's not important. I mention it because I occasionally cite a Met as an example of something, but this is by no means a Mets book.

This is a book about the current state of Major League Baseball (MLB) and how sickening and saddening it's been watching it sink like the *Titanic*. When the *Titanic* crashed into that iceberg, it began sinking very slowly. When the ship eventually broke in half, the remains went down very quickly.

I'm not sure when baseball struck its iceberg. Was it after they invented a stat called saves? Maybe. All I know is baseball broke in half sometime in the last few years, and the joy and dynamic thrill felt when watching it has rapidly plummeted ever since.

I began writing this in April of 2019, but it is now February of 2020. The illegal sign-stealing methods carried out by the Houston Astros and Boston Red Sox have just been confirmed, and it's thrown a wrench into everything. I really don't want to talk about the scandal because, as this book's title indicates, the scandal is not why I wrote this—it is separate from everything else I'm about to discuss. However, I do eventually address it because it is, of course, relevant.

With that now out of the way, let's get on with it.

Baseball doesn't feel like baseball anymore. It's become…distant. Over a relatively short period of time, a few new age thinkers have reshaped baseball into a formulaic shrine that is seemingly worshipped before, during, and after every pitch. The shrine is called "Analytics."

I do not reject analytics. It's considerably important. It provides accurate readings as to how valuable players really are by scientifically examining their performances, and there's no doubt its extensive stat tracking helps devise sensible offensive, defensive, and pitching strategies.

Analytics' value is unmistakable, but the primary focus here is still to cathartically rip it apart from the inside out. Not because there's anything wrong with analytics. There isn't. What's wrong is the blatant *overapplication* of analytics. Today's baseball leaders believe it's all about analytics, but they are mistaken. And because of their misperception, baseball's quality is badly suffering.

During this writing process, one afternoon I drove over to Bill "Mad Dog" Madlock's "Vegas Valley Batter's Box" batting cage in Henderson, Nevada. If you don't know who Bill Madlock is, he was primarily a third baseman who played from 1973 to 1987. A righty, this underrated three-time All-Star who rarely struck out won four batting titles. He racked up over 2,000 hits and had a career batting average (BA) of .305 to go with an .807 on-base plus slugging percentage (OPS).

I went to Madlock's cage, hoping to hear a former major leaguer's thoughts about analytics. Well, I got pretty lucky. When I showed up, Madlock had also just arrived and was sitting down with a newspaper. I told him I was writing a book on how the overuse of analytics is ruining baseball. He just laughed at first. But then, with the delightful cracking sound of bats hitting balls in the background, we talked baseball for an hour. Naturally, he had many things to say, and I will be sharing some of his viewpoints.

The first thing Madlock told me was baseball can never be ruined, no matter how hard analytics tries. I did feel slightly better after hearing that, but the bottom line is that we are in the dark ages of baseball. And since I don't think it's ending any time soon, I've written this for everyone who also can't stand how grossly analytics is overdone. I promise there are no exquisitely calculated formulas, and I only shove a few simple stats down your throat. I'm trying to give statistical bombardment a rest and remember baseball's roots.

Know now that I am not looking to change the minds of those who think analytics should be the basis for essentially every baseball decision. That's probably impossible because these specific people don't really know anything about baseball to begin with. They're good with numbers and stuff, but they don't know *baseball*. Maybe I'm also just another blowhard. But anyone who thinks baseball should revolve around analytics will never grasp what goes on within the game's inner core because of their preoccupation with outer statistics. Analytics covers baseball's exterior quite well. However, it cannot touch the interior because, unlike ballplayers, analytics lacks a heartbeat.

Each time I point out how analytics is overused, I will illustrate what should be done instead. I'll be going over a variety of scenarios, specifically citing rock-bottom examples from the ever-epic 2016 World Series.

I'm also going to draw parallels between baseball and poker. I have been a professional poker player since 2008, mostly living in Las Vegas. I usually play "cash-game" poker, so this is the type of poker I'll be drawing parallels to. In cash games, players can enter and exit the game whenever they want.

To inform everybody who either forgot or never knew, poker is a card game where players compete against each other by betting on their cards' strength. Since poker is played with money, the game is essentially about exposing people's weaknesses. Proper poker involves lots of analytics-type stuff, just like baseball. But for poker's beauty to shine, it must also not become too dependent on it.

This book is nine innings. Innings 1–4 and 6–8 are about analytics, and the 9th inning wraps them up. The 5th inning is a little different. Here I propose changes to certain MLB rules and standards, and I also comment on rule changes that were recently made—some of which directly involve analytics. I included this section because analytics isn't baseball's only dreadfully mishandled element. There are many dopey things Major League Baseball has been keeping in place.

Anyway, to get the analytical ball rolling—sorry, I mean hit out of the ballpark—think of baseball as a house being built and analytics as the tools. Tools are obviously necessary, but the house of baseball needs more than analytics—it is not the twenty-minute brownies makeable in ten minutes it's been cracked up to be.

Besides analytics, you need what front offices, managers, and players once used because it made baseball a dynamically complete game in all facets. I'm talking about intuition.

This book is not meant to be spiritual, or existential, or esoteric, or to have any type of "deepness." However, it is a little hard for me to explain what I think intuition is without sounding at least somewhat spiritual. So, starting now, this book has some deepish moments.

Intuition is absolute intelligence. It is existence itself. All that is in the present moment is all that is intuitive. Intuition led to the creation of analytics because it unlimitedly leads to the creation of everything. Believing otherwise is like trying to take off your underwear before taking off your pants.

As of the end of the 2019 season, the overuse of analytics is still smothering intuition. Intuition has been replaced by statistics and formulas, leaving most in-game decisions preplanned. Baseball has become scripted. *It is not in the moment anymore*, and that is why it's so blandly lifeless now. Suddenly, there is nothing left except a bunch of numbers.

Within just a few seasons, baseball has gone from a world-class improv theater to a daytime soap opera. I know I'll keep watching, no matter how disgusted I get, because I am a very diseased person, but baseball has been reduced to hope—hope that one day it will stop being the ugliest wreckage of something beautiful since the *Titanic*.

1ˢᵀ INNING:
THE MANAGER VERSUS THE HEAD COACH

Baseball is very different from most sports. Hockey, basketball, football, soccer, and many other games play with a clock on a rectangular playing field, and they revolve around the same basic idea: while defending some type of goal on your end of the playing field, move a symmetrically shaped object to the opposition's end and get it in their goal. Baseball is also the only sport that always has a pause and reset between offensive possessions. The defense never suddenly becomes the offense.

With how different baseball is, it isn't random that baseball is the only major sport in which the team's head authority is known as the manager instead of the head coach. This difference is fitting because a manager's responsibilities and actions are not completely synonymous with a head coach's.

For starters, the manager doesn't wear a suit. Baseball moves at such a soothing pace that the skipper dresses like his players. Imagine a manager charging onto the field screaming at an umpire with his tie flapping in the wind. And that's another thing. Only in baseball may the head authority delay the game to argue with an officiator *on* the field.

Head coaches are fully engaged throughout each game. They stand. They pace. They gyrate. They yell. They make substitutions. They craft offensive and defensive strategies. They demonstratively *coach* their players and consult their assistant coaches. Head coaching is high-octane stuff. Today's managers still don't do these things at quite the same level as head coaches. However, the gap has closed significantly, as overusing analytics has produced endless, over-the-top strategizing in and out of the dugout.

Since today's managers are now head coaches trapped inside managers' bodies, I encourage any baseball fan to observe how a manager carries himself today and then watch a game from thirty years ago so they can see the differences. Managers were a lot more reposed back then because baseball was *and still is* that kind of game. Unlike the fast-paced intensity of the other sports, baseball is very slow. These days it's slower than ever, but that is not the cause of today's managers wanting to take on the head coach's intense mentality. It is the effect.

During the 2019 season, announcers began saying baseball is the most difficult game to manage. The untrue absurdity of this declaration borders on unreal, but it is true in the sense that that is what baseball has become. This declaration is the first indication that analytics is overused, because not only is baseball not the most difficult game to manage, it is by far the simplest.

The manager having to handle 162 games is almost twice as many as the next two closest sports (the NHL and NBA seasons each have 82 games), but part of why the baseball season is so long is that the games are mostly composed of inaction. Baseball has no clock, there are hundreds of pauses per game, and once a player is substituted for, he can't return. These three things greatly diminish the urgency for managers to make complex in-game decisions, but they go right on pretending to be head coaches. They still have nothing to do most of the time besides observe, but from the first pitch, you can see how hungry they look. They're just waiting, *waiting*, to make their clever move that'll win that day's battle of analytics. The wheels are constantly turning, and you can see they're thinking, "Hmmm, how should I *manage* this baseball game?"

Once upon a time, the manager made his lineup, handed the ball to his pitcher, parked his ass on the bench, and then watched everything unfold. Sometimes he chewed sunflower seeds, sometimes he chewed gum, and sometimes he chewed tobacco. Sometimes he stood up for a few minutes, and sometimes he said something to his pitcher, catcher, or coaching staff. But for the most part, he kept his mouth shut and his ass stationary.

Things eventually got a little busy. Typically, from the 7th inning on, it was common for the manager to make at least one substitution and sometimes several. The substitutions were usually no-brainers that a monkey could have made. Things like pinch-hitting for the pitcher in a close game, pinch-running for a slowpoke who is carrying the tying or winning run, or bringing in a relief pitcher to replace a clearly fatigued starter. Only occasionally would there be a wonky game that required some real, cagey shrewdness. Apart from those, the manager's two primary duties were keeping the clubhouse spirit harmonized throughout the long season and everyone motivated to hustle. Managing the game was the easy part. Those days are long gone now, though. Overapplying analytics has turned managing into wearing a tuxedo to a Burger King because managers routinely act like they have to "manage" the game.

No matter what analytics uncovers, the manager is still just the manager—he is not a head coach. Therefore, his in-game participation only needs to be what it once was. Managers can continue trying to make baseball sprint underwater, but it is always going to move slowly. As baseball is very monotonous, the manager should be observing more and deciding less.

Since today's managers steadily anticipate chances to apply analytics, they give themselves no opportunity to simply let things "come to them" intuitively—presently. They are thoroughly out of sync with what's actually happening in each game, and this is a big problem.

2ND INNING:
WHO SHOULD BAT SECOND? AND WHERE SHOULD THE PITCHER HIT?

According to analytics, your best hitter should always hit second. No questions such as "Who plays for your baseball team?" are to be asked. All you need to know is fascinatingly simple. Just bat your best hitter second.

Analytics determined that the number-two hitter will wind up with the most runs batted in (RBI) chances, hence why the best hitter should bat second. This strategy is partially in conjunction with another strategy that was devised before analytics became a thing: batting your pitcher eighth instead of ninth. This time, the rationale is having a position player directly precede the top of the order gives your big hitters a better shot at coming up with men on base. When this strategy is applied, the number-nine hitter is sometimes referred to as a "second leadoff hitter."

Most National League (NL) teams haven't done much more than dabble with batting their pitcher eighth, but the senselessness in doing so at all is so extreme that it's hard to believe it was experimented with even one time. Will structuring your batting order so that your worst hitter bats more often always result in failure? No. This isn't about 100 percent versus 0 percent. But using this strategy is a little like saying, "I'm going to buy a tricycle. Then, four weeks later, I will buy a Cadillac. I want to do it this way because if I buy the Cadillac second, I will be upgrading and will enjoy it that much more."

One should not forget that it's not impossible to buy a tricycle and then die before buying a Cadillac. I'm not worried about baseball players dying during a game, but I am worried about a rally dying. And since seeing the pitcher up with two outs and men on base is a miserable feeling, we need to acknowledge that pitchers kill rallies—their offensive prowess is comparable to riding a tricycle to get around. And the higher up in the order pitchers hit, the more chances they will get to end innings.

When the number-eight-hitting pitcher makes the third out, is it nice having a real hitter lead off the next inning in front of your top guys? Yes, *now* it is. But you just had a chance! And the main reason you didn't score was because you intentionally made circumstances easier for the opposition.

Suppose a typical number-eight hitter steps up with runners on second and third base with two outs. He has a weak on-base percentage (OBP) of .295 and an OPS of only .690. The opposing manager wants to just get out of the inning, so he gives the number-eight hitter the intentional walk (IBB) and goes after the pitcher. The pitcher makes out, and the bases are left loaded. That's frustrating for the offense, but at least their leadoff hitter will start the next inning. When the pitcher does get one of his occasional hits, then not only does it come with an extra baserunner aboard, the upcoming leadoff hitter *also* has an extra baserunner to drive in.

Now suppose the pitcher was batting eighth. How will this scenario play out? You'll pitch to the pitcher, and he will most likely make out. But instead of the leadoff hitter starting your next turn at bat, it's your number-nine hitter's measly .295 OBP and .690 OPS. Why is this good?

Suppose the manager (as he often does) takes his chances and goes after a typical number-eight hitter because he wants the pitcher to lead off the next inning. Well, if my number-eight hitter is being pitched to with runners on, I would rather it be any position player in baseball than the pitcher. *So be it* if he makes the last out because, soft hitter or not, position players are still Cadillacs compared to a tricycle pitcher. I never want my pitcher up with men on base.

Getting back to the original question: Regardless of where the pitcher hits, should your number-two hitter be your best hitter? Maybe. I can't know without knowing your personnel. I know that certain teams would be wise to bat their best hitter second on some or all days, but this analytical strategy is not so perfect that it should be universally applied. Why? Because seeing certain hitters in the number-two slot…it just doesn't feel right.

The reasoning I just used is not reasoning at all, and that's why analytics thinkers dismiss this approach. In just a few years, baseball "strategery" has completely shifted. Nearly every decision is now based on analytics exclusively. Logic, intellect, and all of the above have left behind what built baseball: intuition.

LOGIC, ILLOGIC, AND INTUITION

Logic exists because illogic also exists. You can't distinguish one from the other without having both. If you're trying to make a decision or solve a problem (like figuring out who should bat second), it is neither correct nor incorrect to do so logically or illogically. The only mistake you can make with logic or illogic is overrating either one—putting either on a pedestal. Neither is perfect because both are limited. When logic or illogic is put on a pedestal, it is at this point you start asking yourself the wrong questions and doing dumb things. Most of my major blunders have come from overusing illogic, but the opposite is happening in Major League Baseball. Those in charge are so enthralled with the logic of analytics that they've put it on a pedestal. And because of this overallocation, baseball's sensibility and watchability are being extinguished.

In general, logic is overrated, and illogic is underrated because each word has been shallowly assigned a positive or negative connotation. Neither is positive or negative—they're just two ways to approach things. Logic isn't always logical, and illogic isn't always illogical. Using logic isn't absolutely smart—it just means you used logic. Using illogic isn't absolutely imbecilic—it just means you didn't use logic. The two may be opposites, but they are not divided. They work together as two sides of the same coin, and that coin is intuition. Intuition is your inner voice. It is your sixth sense. It talks to you as your friend. It says, "Look! Do this! This belongs here!" Or, "No! Stop! That does not belong there!"

Logic and illogic occur either intuitively, which is natural, or destructively, which is unnatural. The destructive way forces its existence once either gets put on a pedestal. Once the mutual respect for both is lost, the use for whichever approach that was overly praised begins to fade. In other words, insisting on the logic of analytics is bound to turn itself inside out and become illogical because illogic still has to exist. This makes it imperative that analytics be used—but not overused. The computer is to be respected, but objectively. You cannot just crown it king.

Part of what makes a computer a computer is that, unlike people, it's incapable of being conscious. It's only meant to chew on whatever data you feed it. What computers lack in consciousness, they make up for in speed, but the reports computers calculate are not flawless in the sense that they must be treated like conclusive decisions. That is how the analytics thinkers are proceeding, but a computer's calculations are only meant to be contributable to decisions. Logic is only part of the baseball-assessment picture. Illogic completes the other part to make it whole. To maximize success at any walk of life, you're going to have to be illogical at times. But the illogic must occur naturally, intuitively. Otherwise, it's being destructively forced.

When intuitive, you don't "decide" anything. Intuition is a happening rather than a doing. It's a forceless feeling rather than a chosen thought. If you are deciding, you are overthinking. Rather than decide, let your inner voice guide you. Intuition is logical because it doesn't use any logic.

Never mind having expectations from intuition's guidance. Just trust it. Intuition is an airplane, and logic and illogic are its wings. Intuition steers you left or right, regardless of what the outcome is to be. It pulls you like a magnet—nothing forceful, though, because the beauty of intuition is how simple it is. Living intuitively is effortless.

Logic is comprised of intellect, knowledge, explanation, math, science, and whatever else you can think of. All forms of logic encompass each other, and their contributions occur by going to the lab for solutions. Understanding logic can be quite complicated, but it can also be summarized—you can write it down. This is great because you can teach the technical aspects of something to anybody. Anybody can learn facts or formulas to perform a task.

Illogic is nothing like this. It acts with no prior reasoning and never quantifies or explains anything intellectually. Illogic acts from a "just because" standpoint. It is uncomplicated, but it cannot be summarized—you cannot write it down. Illogic might sound ill-advised. But like logic, that is only the case if you overuse it. Then it is occurring egoistically rather than intuitively, and that is never a good sign.

WHAT HAS HAPPENED TO BASEBALL?

I thoroughly get why people have fallen head over heels for analytics or any form of logic. Instead of having to rely on invisible and inexplicable illogical "feelings" to solve problems, they can calculate it logically. Logic provides physical information you can see and touch. You don't have to do what you "think" is a good idea because actual explanations for good ideas exist. Instead of searching for answers in the darkness of illogic, they can be found in the lightness of logic. Logic just seems more real. Illogic gets a bad rap because it seems unreal.

The question is, What feels so real about logic? Well, in the last few years, I've been slowly grasping that living through the mind is unhealthy because it causes endless anguish. Living through the mind seems like something you have to first do in order to eventually stop doing, but whichever way you cut it, we're supposed to direct the mind. The mind is not supposed to direct us, despite how much it tries to. The mind is an amazing tool, but it's the order taker. If a hammer and nails gave you orders, you probably wouldn't obey because the hammer and nails just sit still until you need them. The mind is meant to be used the same way. Once the mind starts running you, enter the madness.

Part of why living through the mind is so nonsensically painful is because it is constantly wrapped up in attaining certainties that do not exist. Analytics thinkers became partial toward analytics because its logic provided the concrete certainty their mind was looking for. But the certain realness of this logic remains false because this partiality is not objective. It's an agenda—something has been put on a pedestal. And once that happens, the preoccupation of having an agenda keeps one from being aware of their intuition—one starts seeing things that aren't there.

Partiality's opposite is, of course, impartiality, and this is not of the mind. It is of the heart because it is objective. With no agenda, one can now be aware of their intuition—one can see what is there. So rather than let your mind direct you, let your intuitive heart do so. The heart is not concerned with certainty because it's only directing right now. It doesn't consider later because it is not certain that later will arrive. Unlike the mind, the heart realizes there will always be uncertainty—that you can never make things completely secure; this is why it is never for or against logic or illogic.

It isn't as such that some people are intuitive, and others are not. Everybody is inherently intuitive, including MLB's players, managers, and executives. You just don't want to *think* about being intuitive because thinking is exactly what intuition is not. Thinking occurs when the mind is running the show. When you are intuitive, you shut the mind up because you're going with your heart's effortless flow.

Learning to use intuition cannot be done externally. It must be done internally because only you can be you. When you are unapologetically yourself, your intelligence is at its peak because intuition is the peak of intelligence. Intuition occurs effortlessly, and nothing feels more effortless than when you're just being you, purely.

If tuning in with intuition seems difficult or unfathomable, it's because you've been trained to be anyone but yourself. The countless imaginary distractions and standards we've been brainwashed to be so sidetracked with squashes one's intuition—one's intelligence. But if you can somehow deprogram all that and just be you, you'll no longer be tied down by logic and its many explanations, and you won't dismiss illogic for its lack of explanation. Whatever you want to do, you will do. You will not batter yourself back and forth with logical or illogical reasons to do or not do something.

Derek Jeter had the highest baseball IQ of anyone I've ever seen. He capitalized on mental lapses all day and almost never had any himself. I don't care what analytics says about his defense because unlike the computer, I actually saw Jeter's whole career. And I simply know that he was reliable in ways no stat could portray. Jeter's baseball intelligence was so high because he was dialed in with his intuition. On the baseball field, he was just himself. Watching him was like watching someone be fully immersed in meditation. It's like he wasn't even there.

Beyond having an intuitive shortstop, I want a manager who is himself. If he is, he'll naturally balance logic and illogic appropriately. Logic seems optimal for the usual and the mundane, but illogic seems optimal for the exceptional. And just as you can't identify logic without also identifying illogic, you can't identify what is mundane without identifying what is not.

If a manager is permitted to be himself, then not only will he adeptly handle all situations, the team will also play in his image. They will become absorbed in his identity, and this will elevate their output. Today, there is hardly any identity among managers because they're all basically the same. They are all directed exclusively by the logic of analytics, so baseball has subsequently taken on a deathly predictable repeat.

Believe it or not, I really do love the intellect of analytics and sabermetrics. When I look up a player, I immediately check his Wins Above Replacement (WAR). Every team has players who get more or less respect than they deserve, and I'm thrilled there are advanced stats to tell us more about what's going on because it limits how often we overrate or underrate players.

Nevertheless, analytics cannot be every meal of every day, like the lifetime prison sentence the analytics thinkers are making us serve. I like ketchup on hot dogs, but I'm not about to put it on pancakes. The analytics thinkers have gotten so carried away with the "certainty" of logic they have turned baseball into a clogged toilet. They use it for everything. It's become a crutch. Baseball's spontaneously intuitive creativity has been replaced by repetitively manufactured intellect. Fans hate it, and it's not because we're missing something. This isn't about us living in the past, clinging to overvalued archaic stats. No. We are simply sensing that what we're seeing is flat-out idiotic, and it's hard not to because the overuse of analytics is that conspicuous. Let us be thankful for analytics, but it must be acknowledged that it's being gorged way too much. And because of this obesity, baseball is being sent backward.

JACK MCKEON

In 2003, the Marlins held a 3–2 World Series lead over the Yankees. Entering Game 6, Marlins manager Jack McKeon elected to pitch his twenty-three-year-old starter Josh Beckett on only three days' rest in Yankee Stadium. When asked why he didn't want the steady Mark Redman for Game 6 and Beckett on regular rest for a potential and decisive Game 7, the seventy-two-year-old McKeon said something like, "Strange things happen in Game 7 at Yankee Stadium."

Now what the hell kind of a logical and intellectual explanation is that? This is what the *manager* had to say? What's the logic? There is none. It's illogical—and that's the point. McKeon didn't skip Mark Redman for Game 6 because he got lit up his last two postseason starts (including at Yankee Stadium in Game 2). He skipped him because he wanted no part of Game 7. He wasn't interested in "playing it safe" by saving Beckett for the next day. Short rest or not, Beckett felt like the best man to seal the deal that night, so he was getting the ball.

How did Beckett do against all the pressure of Yankee Stadium and the hype of pitching on short rest? How about a 2–0 five-hit shutout to bring home the championship! Beckett surrendered a leadoff double in the 7th inning, and a leadoff single in the 8th inning, but McKeon didn't automatically replace him like today's managers undoubtedly would have.

McKeon all but conceded the Marlins would have lost Game 7 if they didn't win Game 6, which was why he wasn't willing to do what "the book" said and save Beckett. Rather than have a logical excuse for losing, he took an illogical shot at winning. And rightfully so—because how many times have you wanted to strangle a head coach or manager because he wouldn't do something exceptional in an exceptional situation? You knew he would be afraid to face the media if an unusual risk failed him. You knew he knew that as long as he takes a conventional route that has been approved by the logic of "the book," then failing is okay.

McKeon's decision seemed so risky because he dove into the unknown headfirst. He had no documented logic to deludedly lull him into thinking that he, with certainty, could not possibly be making a mistake. He simply went with an impulse that said it's time to deviate from the norm. And like distinguishing logic from illogic, you need something besides the norm to have a norm to identify. If no one ever deviated from the norm, there wouldn't be a norm at all because no one is deviating from it.

I'm not praising McKeon's decision because it worked. I'm praising it because of why he made it. He fearlessly followed his intuition instead of just sticking with the logical "safety" of the norm. He didn't care how moronic others would think he was if his strategy failed, and I wouldn't think any less of his decision if Beckett had gotten knocked out in the 1st inning. Intuition won't always lead you to what you had in mind—but that's okay. As long as you trust intuition, you will stay maximally intelligent and get to where you are supposed to go at maximal efficiency.

GAME THEORY OPTIMAL

If you drive a car off a five-hundred-foot cliff, the car has been misused because cars don't fly. If you apply analytics to every baseball decision without even a hesitation, no less an exception, analytics has been misused. Maximizing the use of anything depends on knowing when not to use it as much as when to use it. If a pitcher throws nothing but curveballs, it won't be as effective as it would be if he had another pitch to complement it.

This concept also directly applies to the game of poker. Like baseball, poker has intensely and immensely changed in recent years. Internet poker really shook things up because it opened the door to intellectually discovering unbeatable strategies.

Game Theory Optimal (GTO) is a complex strategy system designed to play poker in a manner that cannot be exploited. It provenly *guarantees* victory, but by what margin?

Poker players should only use a complex strategy like GTO as often as they are playing a complex opponent. If they are playing a simple (weak) opponent, they should use a simple strategy. What is a simple strategy? Using an approach that reveals tendencies. That sounds catastrophic, but you have to look closer.

If I stepped into the batter's box against a major league pitcher, he'll know I'm a simple opponent and go after me with a simple strategy. He won't nibble the corners or try to fool me with breaking pitches. He'll just rear back and fire in his fastball because there's no need to get fancy when pitching to someone who isn't a baseball player. Throwing me all fastballs seems exploitable because I know what's coming, but it doesn't matter because I can't exploit it. If I were a baseball player, now the pitcher must use a more complex strategy because getting a baseball player to fail is much harder.

Hitters going from the minor leagues to the major leagues often have a difficult time adjusting because the pitchers are more complex. In the minors, you'll probably get the fastball when you're in a fastball count. It's relatively predictable. It's simple. It's exploitable. When you're in the majors, you're much likelier to get any pitch during any count. It's far less predictable. It's complex. It's not easily exploited. Most minor leaguers can't hit a curveball, but most major leaguers can. Major league hitters are tougher to retire because their hitting skills make them more complex. That is why pitchers need more than one quality pitch in their repertoire.

When I'm playing poker against poker players, I can't just throw fastballs because they are going to hit them. It's crucial I use a complex strategy and be that much more conscious about how I'm playing. When I'm playing with people who are just playing poker, I *shouldn't* play as complexly. I should play more exploitatively—more illogically. Pouring in fastballs right down the pipe isn't as dangerous because the likelihood of them hitting them is small enough that it's worth the risk.

Not every pro poker player would agree though. Some pros use GTO no matter the opponent, and by doing so, they're leaving money on the table. A poker player who depends on GTO is the same as someone who thinks all baseball decisions should be made in accordance with analytics. Each believes in their logical strategy so heavily that intuition winds up a nonfactor. Illogic is never used, but it still destructively occurs due to logic's overuse.

Overusing GTO is the same as throwing me a curveball when I'm in the batter's box. You don't need to because I can't hit the fastball, the curveball is more taxing on your arm, and it's more likely to miss the strike zone. Overusing GTO limits how much money you can win because you could be winning more if intuition was also partaking.

By being preplanned, analytics and GTO ignore the presence of *now*. This is fine until you start refusing to take any time to notice current circumstances and consider making exceptions. Overusing a strategy means you're being too consistent. Consistency is great, but inconsistency is necessary because circumstances are also inconsistent.

The players who only use GTO do it for the same reason an analytics thinker refuses to ignore the computer. They feel stupid doing something illogical, something that their calculations wouldn't agree with. Even though they (probably) know their opponent is unlikely to know when there's an opportunity to exploit, they still feel they are making a mistake and don't want to risk exposure. They've gotten comfortable with the supposed "certainty" of their system and feel uncomfortable doing something that doesn't have a quantified explanation attached to it.

If that's not the only reason why, then it's also because they haven't tuned in with how to read other players. This is unfortunate because being able to sense when an opponent is strong or weak is a *brutally* effective skill. It is most definitely well worth developing because it makes a poker player that much more dynamic and unpredictable. And as long as people have reactions to winning, losing, making strong hands, or not making strong hands, they are capable of being read.

In complex games like poker and baseball, there are only so many simple solutions that constantly yield maximum success. Just like every baseball situation can, every poker hand versus every opponent can require a unique course of action. Can you lean on the solutions of GTO and still make money? Sure. Can you lean on the solutions of analytics and still win? A hundred percent yes. But why settle for winning $80 an hour if you can win $102 by letting intuition weigh in? Why settle for scoring 4.4 runs a game when you can score 4.6 by letting intuition weigh in as to who should bat second? Or anywhere?

If you're only going to use GTO, then it doesn't even matter who your opponent is. But a poker player should always consider their opponent. Of the many details within a poker hand, none are greater than who the opponent is because that's where all the other details stem from! That's why the wildest, most outside-the-box, most illogical decisions made by poker players usually occur against exploitable opponents. Exploitable opponents are exploitable because it is worth it to let yourself be exploitable. And the best poker players know they need to gamble some with these weak players. They know to take some unorthodox chances because they know weak players make so many bizarre mistakes. They know that versus these particular opponents, logic isn't completely logical, and illogic isn't completely illogical.

What's interesting about exploitable opponents is they aren't *always* weak players—sometimes savvy opponents become exploitable. There are plenty of pros and other regular players in Las Vegas. As you log more and more hours with them, you learn about each other's style. And the longer the same styles continue, the greater the possibility of exploitation there is...

You could be a tight player who seldom bluffs, especially for big money, but now you're in a hand with a great player who you have strong reason to believe (be it for logical or illogical reasons) holds a hand he won't continue with unless he thinks you could be bluffing. This you don't fear, though, because your opponent has never seen you fire a big bluff in all the hours you've played together.

We'll say this is a situation you'd ordinarily never bluff in because it looks too suspicious. It's exploitable—you know the story you are trying to tell will fail to logically convince most players, strong or weak. But when you have enough conservative history with a player (especially a competent, disciplined one) who you feel has both a weak hand and no suspicions of you, you can exploit him by making a sudden illogical move—because you know this player knows how unprofitable it is to try and call bluffs against opponents who never seem to do it. The illogic is so illogical it becomes logical. Now in the event the strong opponent somehow figures out what has happened and *still* calls your bluff, then so be it. You were outmastered.

I have no doubt this exact same battle of cat-and-mouse goes on between pitchers and hitters who have been facing each other for years. Surely, they adjust by remembering what pitches were thrown in previous at-bats (ABs) and what the results were. This is why watching a great hand between two advanced poker players reminds me of watching a great AB between a star hitter and a star pitcher.

Illogic is going to have its moments of outright failure in poker because, like logic, it's also limited. But if not overused, it'll prevail far more than leave you looking unbelievably half-witted for doing something so heavily against conventional wisdom.

The only way to overuse illogic is forcing it—if you put it on a pedestal. Then it is no longer what you think because you're using it for fear-based reasons—you think nothing else will work. This happens when a poker player or baseball manager forcefully *wants* to read an opponent or situation a certain way instead of just letting the read happen intuitively, objectively.

Anything that is done forcefully is destructive. So just be intuitive; be yourself. When intuition strikes you to do something logical, do it. When it strikes you to do something illogical, do it. Don't question illogic in favor of the limited logic you've gathered from all the knowledgeable explanations you've memorized.

ANOTHER EXAMPLE

In a poker hand, sometimes you'll find yourself in a spot where 85 to 90 percent of the time you have the losing hand. You're facing a big bet. You know GTO says just fold (voluntarily lose) and move on. The analytics thinkers would feel the same way.

The difference is that if you're tapped in with your intuition and therefore are not partial toward logic or illogic, you can feel it when you're in that 10 to 15 percent. There's nothing else to do or contemplate when an intuitive bolt hits you because the work is already done. So, as long as you don't care that what you're sensing is inexplicable, you'll have no struggle following the impulse. The GTO and analytics obsessed would say you made a mistake and were fortunate. Wrong. You were masterful. And part of what makes masters masterful is they can do things you can't imagine. They are experts at things you never knew existed.

It's unusual when a 10-to-15-percent scenario comes up, but it would be quite unusual if a 10-to-15-percent scenario never came up. As mentioned before, abnormal circumstances seem to be when illogic has its greatest impact. Defining *unusual* is subjective, but as things can't only occur in a usual manner (otherwise, there would be no usual manner), you shouldn't always aim for what's logical. Logic is great. But overdoing it will destroy you the same way overdoing analytics is destroying baseball.

BALANCE

Suppose you have one hundred decisions, and ninety-two are best made logically. Since illogic and logic can only function when both are properly applied, this means they share equal importance. The average importance of each of the ninety-two logical decisions will be relatively low because there are so many of them, and the average importance of each of the eight illogical decisions will be relatively high because there are so few of them. You don't want to mess up the logical decisions because their need occurs so frequently, but you also don't want to mess up the illogical ones because their need occurs so infrequently.

You can ride poker's stakes as high as you want if you ace GTO and never do anything illogical. However, you will never dominate each level of stakes for as much money as possible. On the flip side, playing primarily exploitable strategies will work against exploitable opponents, but you'll never get out of the small stakes because you don't know GTO's fundamentals. The bigger the game, the more necessary logic is because the competition is tougher. But no matter how big the game is, knowing GTO is mandatory all the same, as knowing what analytics advises.

When I moved to Vegas, I had no logical outline besides knowing what stakes my bankroll was big enough for. I set no goals regarding hours, winnings, anything. I hadn't as a part-time player, and it still didn't cross my mind to formulate a plan as a full-time player because I trusted I'd be fine. I used logic when it felt right and illogic when that felt right. I balanced the two by not being partial toward either one. I obviously had my hiccups, but I didn't insist on having answers before circumstances had a chance to reveal themselves. Baseball should handle analytics the same way.

Batting your best hitter second is more applicable in the American League (AL) because of the designated hitter (DH). However, DH or not, managers need to know their players as much as analytics. Maybe the best guy to bat second on a given day is the best hitter, but maybe it isn't. Maybe the roster does not have someone who should always bat second. Just experiment! That's part of what spring training is for—seeing what flows through trial and error, seeing what gels spontaneously and thoughtlessly, while always remembering to communicate with the players. Everyone talks about how important communication is, so why make baseball a computer program? If managers let themselves act intuitively rather than insist on logic or illogic, they'll bat the right guy second.

BILL MADLOCK ON THE NUMBER-TWO HITTER

Madlock talked about how it's a mistake to see guys like Aaron Judge, Kris Bryant, and other top well-rounded power hitters be regularly slated in the number-two slot and about how even though batting second will get them more ABs, they should still bat third or fourth so they can drive in more runs. As it is, we're seeing more and more guys with high home-run totals but low RBI totals. In 2019, a whopping twelve players hit at least 30 home runs while driving in fewer than 80. Madlock said if you're hitting that many home runs, you need to be driving in at least 100 runs.

To me, Aaron Judge is the most extreme example of someone who should not be hitting second. It makes me wonder what the Mets lineup of the late '90s and early 2000s would have looked like if their scariest hitter, Mike Piazza, hit second. The mere thought of that sounds strange, and I doubt it would have improved anything, especially considering how good a number-two hitter Edgardo Alfonzo was. This brings back the idea that determining your number-two hitter should be based on whom you're working with rather than exclusively on who your biggest threat is. The Yankees have strung together some great years recently, but their October eliminations have mostly been because their bats went silent. That could have easily still happened if Judge wasn't the number-two hitter, but the Yankees have multiple options for the number-two slot. I would try Gleyber Torres. But whoever they use, it shouldn't be Judge. He is too devastating to waste at the top of the order. And every time he steps up in the 1st inning as the number-two hitter, it just doesn't feel like it's time to see him yet.

3ʀᴅ INNING:
THE STARTING PITCHER IS DOMINATING, BUT WE'RE STILL GOING TO THE BULLPEN

Growing up in the '90s, the best part of the day was seeing the newspaper with all the previous day's box scores laid out and waiting for me on the kitchen table. I'd always been beyond crazy about baseball, and my dad, a steady early riser, always made sure I saw the results.

One memory from those box scores was often seeing no more than three pitchers used per game, per team. Only when a team used at least five pitchers did it start to seem like a lot. When exactly three pitchers were used, the starter didn't necessarily pitch seven innings. They often went deeper into games, but it wasn't shell-shocking to see a reliever who wasn't the closer pitch more than one inning.

The New York Times box scores also included everybody's pitch count. It was unusual to see any starting pitcher throw fewer than 100 pitches in a halfway decent start, and 115–120 was normal. Only when a pitch count got to around 130 did it seem exceptionally high.

I don't want to see starting pitchers empty the clip every start or pitch 300 innings a season like they once did. But the most aggravating part of analytics' overuse is how often it leads to starting pitchers getting taken out of games when they're calmly in control—when they're dominating.

The idea of having a ferocious 9th inning fireballer come in and finish the game started before the '90s. However, this decade is when it practically became a constitutional amendment that you use no one *but* your closer in the 9th inning. How many times did I see a starting pitcher roll through eight innings and then get taken out because it was a save situation? I wanted to break something every time. I didn't care if the closer struck out the side on nine pitches. I detested the automatic thoughtlessness of removing a dominant pitcher for absolutely no reason besides "Now it's time to bring in the closer." But, my goodness, what I would give now to have those days back!

WATCHING IS IMPORTANT

It's all but factual that the worst-managed game in baseball history belongs to Joe Maddon in Game 7 of the 2016 World Series. This also makes his winding up on the winning side the luckiest thing to ever happen to anybody. Maddon couldn't even give away the Cubs' first ring in 108 years. And how fittingly ironic that the time they most deserved to lose, they won.

The worst part is it just *happened* to be Joe Maddon managing. There is only so much to knock on him specifically because so many other managers, if not all of them, would have done exactly what he did—or things even more asinine.

Before Joe Maddon's popularity perhaps went to his head, I loved him when he managed in Tampa Bay. The Rays always showed up with some no-name-looking team and then proceeded to be a huge pain in the ass.

This is of course why Maddon became a big name, but for me, there was more to it. Maddon's energy was awesome. I loved the way he carried himself in the dugout. He radiated such an assured expertise, and the Rays' results reflected *him*, not the other way around.

An analytics thinker could have never told me anything like that because analytics thinkers believe every baseball truth lies only within the statistics. They are certain observing doesn't tell you very much—that you can't sense how well somebody is performing or will perform just by watching. On the contrary: *oh, yes, you can*. And because computers don't know what intuition is, analytics thinkers are of no arrogant authority to deny its most relevant existence.

Watching and observing is not exactly a novel way of figuring out a baseball player's worth. For years, that's how it was done because there was only so much logic to fall in love with. Illogic had to be used regularly. And as time went on, baseball people gradually figured out what was logical because they followed intuition. Intuition is the path to discovery. It is the moment. It is intelligence's nucleus. This is the biggest reason you cannot bow down to analytics. By doing so, you are killing off where baseball came from. If intuition can discover analytics, then it should be given the opportunity to say, "Don't use analytics."

It isn't though. Most analytics diehards are now so taken by the numbers, they are convinced that *it is not necessary* to watch the players play, that all they have to do is run their calculations and a dependable report on that player's value will be composed. *Wwwhhhaaaaatttttt?*

Out of all the lines overusing analytics crosses, this one is the most violating. To even think of something as nonsensical as that is the dumbest, most ridiculous, and inexcusable conviction. It is pure stuck up laziness and sets a terrible example for work ethic. You don't need to watch the players play? Oh boy. There's trying to reinvent the wheel, and then there's this. This is no different than looking at twenty different job résumés and then filling the position based on whose is the most impressive.

It doesn't matter what analytics is capable of. To fully understand what you have, you have to watch everyone play, the same as you have to conduct job interviews. You have to actually *see* and be present with what you are dealing with before deciding which players to assign to what level, or trade, or anything. Analytics helps assemble a winning team, but it tells you nothing about a player's instinct, how coachable he is, his gumption, what kind of a teammate he might be—anything and everything else.

Bill Belichick coaches football, but I'd like to see someone tell him and all his Super Bowl rings that he doesn't need to see his players play. One of the many reasons Belichick has won so much is there are things he doesn't put up with. He doesn't care how talented you are or how much you have already contributed. If you show yourself in any way to be selfish or foolish, *you're cut*. For Belichick, being a professional entails that you actually *be* professional. I know Belichick has been behind some illegal activity, but that's irrespective of how much he intelligently demands this humility from his players.

I don't know how intelligent any of the analytics people are, but I do know they are using their strategy in a very unintelligent way because of how goofily they misapply it. They effectively treat analytics like it's Bugs Bunny. It bats in all nine spots and plays all nine positions. Bugs Bunny is a great cartoon character, but baseball is not.

THE 2016 WORLD SERIES

Trailing the series 3–1 with one last home game, the Cubs forced the series back to Cleveland with a tight-knit, come-from-behind 3–2 victory in Game 5. Facing demise, Cubs closer Aroldis Chapman turned in a most necessary eight-out save. He threw 42 pitches, which is around two to four times the number he'd normally throw.

After the off day, things got very peculiar in Game 6. The Cubs jumped on Josh Tomlin early and took a sizable 7–2 lead into the 6th inning. Cubs starting pitcher Jake Arrieta hadn't been coasting, but he was bulldogging his way through as usual. After retiring the first two hitters, his 102nd pitch resulted in a walk, and Joe Maddon promptly took him out. I disagreed with this move, but I'm not going to split hairs over it, as it was nothing compared to the lunacy that happened later.

In came the lefty Mike Montgomery. He took the Cubs into the 7th inning and got a couple of outs. But after a second runner reached base, Aroldis Chapman was brought in again. What?

The strangest part about asking Chapman to get seven more outs was the fact he wasn't brought into a save situation. Every baseball fan knows the Eleventh Commandment, which says, "Thou shall not bring in your closer unless it's a save situation."

Chapman definitely had to be extensively used in Game 5, so I give Maddon maximum credit for that. But here? Why? The Cubs had *five* other relief pitchers! If you're not going to use them up five runs, then why are they on the postseason roster?

I get that the Cubs are still facing elimination and that they can't play Game 7 before they win Game 6, but they were up five runs with the eighth-best bullpen ERA in baseball! Joe Maddon should have been jumping for joy! But instead of avoiding Chapman, Maddon analytically went to him again. Since he's his best reliever, he figured he can just ask him to be the middle reliever and the closer.

PITCH COUNT

Pitch count is often both over- or underemphasized, and the overuse of analytics has created the daily garbage that we see. A starting pitcher is seldom allowed to throw more than 100 pitches or go through the batting order a third time for fear of ineffectiveness. But relievers, especially closers, are treated invincibly. Their pitch count apparently means nothing. Somehow, they carry an infinite supply of stamina. No heavy workload is feared to affect their future effectiveness. When their preplanned inning to enter the game arrives, they come in and are left out there to *die* if that's what it takes because we depend on the reliever—a *bench pitcher* who wasn't good enough to be a starter.

Starting pitchers are rarely stretched beyond their preplanned pitch count even when a no-hitter is intact. Ross Stripling of the Dodgers had one going in his major league debut on April 8, 2016. With one out in the 8th inning, his 100th pitch was his fourth walk of the game. Manager Dave Roberts instantly took him out, and the bullpen quickly blew the 2–0 lead.

It doesn't matter that the bullpen lost the game. This is modern-day baseball—the reliever gets the benefit over the starter. Why? Because after learning that the bullpen had a lower ERA than starting pitchers after a certain point, the analytics thinkers decided in a most oversimplified manner, "Okay, once we reach this point, we're taking the starter out, no matter how he's doing."

They fail to realize that this information, though good to know, is still only a factor. That every situation remains independent of statistics. That what is going on *right now* is what's most important. It's like any poker hand. A hand I should normally play a certain way doesn't mean I always will because at any particular time, circumstances might be different.

Dave Roberts repeated this act during the 2017 World Series. Game 4 starter Alex Wood was mowing down the Astros in Houston. With two outs and nobody on in the 6th inning, the ever-talented George Springer homered off of a *slightly* hanging slider. It was Houston's first hit and only Wood's 84th pitch, but, because of the script, statistics, and overall lack of concern for overusing relief pitchers, Roberts took Wood right out. Brandon Morrow entered, and the Dodgers won 6–2, but that loony 13–12 extra-inning affair happened the next day. In that Game 5, Morrow threw six pitches, recorded no outs, and gave up four hits, including two home runs.

When a starting pitcher is rolling the way Stripling and Wood were, you'd think the manager would think, "I like my job today. All I have to do is sit here and watch."

Nope. Rather than let the domination be, like managers previously did those other thousands of times, today's managers insist on analytics and the preplanned relievers. They bring them into games when it's completely unnecessary, and slowly but surely, they are getting overtaxed. Then finally comes a day where they do need them, and suddenly they get slammed. Analytics thinkers just hardheadedly write it off. They say, "Okay, it happens sometimes."

Morrow pitched in every game of that World Series and seven of the eight postseason games prior to it. It's nice he had a great regular season, but that doesn't mean he must be used in every postseason game. As hitters are expected to gain an advantage from repeatedly facing the same starting pitcher, it's also to be expected when the same reliever comes in day after day after day. Call Morrow's Game 5 meltdown unlucky if you insist, but this is an inevitable result from overuse. Yes, the Astros were stealing signs, and that lessens this example's value, but blaming it on that is a little extreme considering how regularly we see stuff like this.

It wasn't that long ago that pitch count wasn't even posted on the score overlay on TV. Now it gets mentioned almost every inning. You also see more hits coming on 0–2 pitches because starting pitchers know they can't afford to be crafty. They can't throw strategic "waste pitches" when ahead in the count because they are given so little room to do their job. They are forced to go after hitters if they have any hopes of pitching deep into games and earning a nice contract.

Bill Madlock reminded me that part of why teams quickly pull starters even when they're cruising is that they just want to protect them from injury—this was the case when Dave Roberts pulled out Ross Stripling. I like that teams are favoring health over personal feats, but throwing overhand is unnatural. Pitching is very hard on the body, *period*. Injuries aren't going anywhere, no matter what you do, so you might as well stretch a pitcher when he's performing at his peak. There is no question that pitchers can be stretched because they were for decades. They're just never asked to anymore because of analytics.

THE GLORY

Every team in every sport has at least one backup for every position—except for the closer. Another reliever or two might pick up a handful of saves during the season, but not because they were the formal backup. Maybe the closer wasn't available that day. Maybe he blew the save or already pitched in a tie game. Whatever the reason, it wasn't because of matchups or, heaven forbid, to relieve a closer who clearly had *nothing* that day. The closer is *hands down* the most glorified and overhyped position in sports, and it's because he doesn't have a backup.

There are hardly any closers worth trading for or giving huge contracts to. Closers come and go so frequently, you'd probably be aghast as to how many you've forgotten in the last twenty years. Relief pitchers are very unreliable, which is why they are such a year-to-year commodity.

Just about every bullpen should be a bullpen by committee. Every reliever should be able to enter every inning and situation because of how much matchups can vary. Relievers are so hyped up, so let them live up to their billing. Don't give me that stupid, lame, petty, and pathetic argument of, "The toughest three outs to get in the game are the last three," as to why only one guy should be slamming the door. This is Major League Baseball. If you are incapable of getting "the toughest three outs" because you are too mentally soft, then you shouldn't be in the majors. We see the batting order get jumbled up all the time. Why can't you do that with the bullpen? Why is there a "pitching order"? Why is it, oh-so-stubbornly, "You pitch this inning, then this guy pitches, then this guy pitches, and then this guy pitches"?

If you want to have a main guy to finish games, fine. But have someone else getting loose when he enters the 9th inning *just in case* he stinks. It's not blasphemy. We constantly see multiple relievers per inning before the 9th inning, but the 9th inning approach is completely different, and it's because of the stat called "saves." The save is the reason closers are so glorified. "Saving" the game sounds heroic—as if the game could have never been won if not for the almighty closer's saviorhood. Time and time again, you'll see a closer who looks nothing like he usually does, and then the TV network emphasizes the glorious melodrama by showing the empty bullpen. "It's all on his shoulders." Oh, how exciting.

Leaving in closers and removing starting pitchers at a certain time, no matter how either is doing, further shows how baseball has completely thrown away the presence of *now* and thus the use of intuition. Running a baseball game isn't about clicking this button or that button at this time or at that time. It's just about sizing up what's in front of you *right now* so that intuition can guide you. Automatically going to the bullpen at whatever time is no different than saying, "I don't have a headache, but I'm going to take Tylenol now because it's five o'clock."

FIREMEN

There's something amazing about the pitcher. Football has the quarterback, soccer and hockey have the goalie, and baseball has the pitcher. These players are the queens on the chessboard. They have the most direct ability to have the biggest impact on the game's outcome.

The starting pitcher is your frontline warrior. He's the first man into battle, carrying the team with his blood and guts. This is why it is really great when a starting pitcher throws a complete game. Not only does he let the bullpen rest, he also provides a great boost for the team's morale, which you can legitimately feel after he gets the last out.

Those days are few and far between now though. The newly discovered intellect says, "Don't let your starter face the opposing lineup more than two times because it becomes increasingly advantageous for the hitters." If a starter is allowed to start the 7th, or the 6th, or even the 5th inning, his only shot at staying in is if he's flawless the rest of the way. If someone reaches base so much as via a swinging bunt, he's pulled. It's as though the analytics thinkers cannot grasp that maybe there's nothing wrong if someone reaches base, that maybe the starting pitcher can still be effective in the later innings even if he isn't performing flawlessly.

A dominating starting pitcher has earned the trust and chance to keep going. It's not that I have to see him get bombed before replacing him. I'm just not favoring someone who hasn't thrown a pitch over the guy who's been producing the whole game. Relief pitchers are firemen. Their job is to put out fires. Yet the fire department continuously receives phone calls from the dugout even when there's no fire—only a cat stuck in a tree.

An unquantifiable, intuitive problem with removing a cruising starting pitcher is that it dents the team's momentum. Here they were, being led by their starter barreling his way through the game. They're all behind him, pushing forward collectively. Then suddenly, he's out. A reliever comes in, and then he gets pulled. Then another. And then another. Increasing how much time the players spend standing around waiting for a new pitcher slows them down momentously. Momentum builds as a starter dominates deep into a game. The team becomes empowered. I know this because I'm one of those weird people who still watches the games. I'm one of those dummies who still believes if they watch the game, they might notice something important.

MYSTIQUE

There's something very mysterious about watching a great athlete get into a groove. There's really a great mystery to watching any competitor or performer do what they do when they're completely dialed in.

When you enter this space, it's like you're not even there because you have totally lost yourself in the art of your activity. Everything you do effortlessly flows without thought. Some people call this space "the zone."

An athlete isn't only in the zone when performing flawlessly. He can still strike out, hit into a double play, make an error, or walk someone. He also isn't in the zone when he appears to be performing flawlessly because there can always be some luck involved. A bloop can fall in for a hit, the wind can turn a fly ball into a home run, or someone can hit a frozen rope right into the third baseman's glove. This is why you have to watch. When you look at stats, you can see what's happened. When you watch, you can see what's happening. This difference is significant.

It's amazing to watch someone be in the zone because, unless you're preoccupied with something else (like analytics), you can't miss it once they've entered it. Anyone objectively paying attention can intuitively feel the rhythm the performer is feeling and knows to just leave them be—not to mention that as a manager, opponent, teammate, and fan, it's inspiring to sit back and just enjoy the performer's mastery. Even when a pitcher is shutting a team down, some of the opposing hitters are in total admiration, awe, and appreciation of what's happening.

Analytics is more effective for handling ordinary circumstances than exceptional ones because analytics cannot comprehend that some days a starting pitcher just *has it*, and some days he doesn't. Analytics guarantees nothing because you don't know what's going to happen any particular day—hence why you have to watch.

A dominating pitcher can throw more effective pitches than his routine number. Maybe he's normally good for 110 pitches, but it'll take 130 to gas him on a dominant day. When a pitcher is in command, the manager just needs to *chill*, and his intuition will tell him to if he objectively lets it. By not putting analytics on a pedestal, he will understand his pitcher's fuel tank is exceptionally large today. He, of course, still has to keep an eye on him because of how quickly things can change, but until a zoned pitcher starts showing signs that his groove is beginning to fade, you don't even think about the bullpen! And you especially don't go to the bullpen the moment someone reaches first base or hits one ball hard! If the manager suspects the tides are beginning to turn, his next step is visiting the mound to find out more about what's going on.

A pitcher who doesn't have it will throw fewer effective pitches than his routine number. When this is happening, the manager shouldn't wait long to yank him because his fuel tank is exceptionally small. If and when he starts to show any signs of settling in, only then should the manager consider stretching him. What he shouldn't do is leave a sitting duck out there giving the game away because he wants to save his bullpen from getting a few extra outs. Modern baseball leaders basically have everything backward. None of them get that you empty your eight-man bullpen when the starter is getting *shelled*. Not when he's shining! It's no different than working out. Have you never pushed yourself harder because you felt extra strong? Have you never ended a workout early because you felt crappy? It's fine to have a general plan going in, but you should always be flexibly willing to deviate from it.

As a fan, there is nothing more demoralizing than seeing a cruising starter be taken out. You all but know whoever is coming in is going to blow the game, and then he flushes it down the toilet faster than you can blink. When you pull a grooving starter, the opposition rejoices. They think, "Yes! Thank you! We have a shot!"

Doesn't competition include not making your opponent happy? Whenever the best player comes off the field, a momentum shift takes place for the opposition.

How many times have we all heard not to fix what isn't broken, not to overthink, and to keep things simple? Cliché or not, this advice did not come around for nothing, because doing otherwise is how things get overcomplicated. Every time you bring in a new pitcher, *you are starting over*. You have no idea if the new guy will have it or not. And when you use seven pitchers, it is far likelier that one will have a bad game than if you had only used three.

Every time a reliever makes an appearance, you are getting closer to his next bad game. If you already have a starting pitcher who is on cruise control and showing zero signs of fatigue, why would you ever want to take him out? If there's someone to push, it's the starter—not the reliever. Perfect games are rare, but perfect-game stuff is not. When a guy is rolling, don't preemptively decide to start over with a reliever, because you have no idea how he'll do! A reliever's expected value may be proven by his stats, but his expected value is not as concrete as the current pitcher's because he's already demonstrated his day's value with 60-100 pitches!

Like pitching, poker is also not a nine-to-five job. I never play a set number of hours. When I sit down, I don't know when I'm getting up because each session's length always depends on a few things. Some days are great opportunities. A lot of my opponents are weak, and for whatever reason that doesn't need to be logically summarized, I feel extra sharp too—no apprehensiveness, just appropriately aggressive because I'm in the mood for action. I feel at ease in the game flow, and time is flying. Win or lose, these days I play ten to sixteen hours because the best feeling for a poker player is not winning—it is knowing when he's in a good game. A good game literally feels good to be in. Nothing is greater than when I get to tell myself, "All right, I'm going to sit in this chair, and I am not getting up any time soon."

Other days aren't so fruitful. Most of my opponents are not overwhelmingly profitable to play against, and I feel...*icky*. My play feels sluggishly fatigued, the action is dragging, and I'm easily distracted by my phone. Win or lose, these days I'm out of there within two to four hours. Then, depending on how I feel, I'll either go home or play somewhere else.

I've never kept stats on how I do in, say, hours one through five or six through ten of sessions. And if I did, those numbers would still only be a factor. They would not be held greater than what's currently happening, so they wouldn't automatically determine how long I should play. If I'm playing well against a lineup full of opponents with whom I match up well, then I continue playing. End of story.

Assessing my stamina and ability to perform should be easier than assessing another person's, but either way, this is why you need a manager who will let himself sense when a pitcher looks exceptionally good or bad. Since analytics and intuition are both essentially trying to make predictions, the best strategy is to not be partial toward either one. You don't have to pick one or the other. Instead, just let them share roles as balanced friends who complement each other. Watch what's happening, be aware of the numbers, and listen to intuition. It might say go with analytics; it might not. Either way, intuitive choices are never "decisions" because intuitive living is simply letting yourself go in whatever direction the stream of life takes you.

THE MEANS

Another problem with the false certainty of analytics is that it expects everyone to perform to their means, and this *clearly* does not happen every day. Competitors have their good days, bad days, and medium days.

Suppose a starter makes three starts. In the first two games, he is dominant through six innings. He goes out for the 7th inning and gets them 1-2-3 both times. In the third start, things are shakier. His pitch count through six innings is still comparable to the prior two starts, but his work seems less rhythmic this time. He's battling more than he's sailing. But, okay, he still gets another crack since he was great in the 7th inning the last two times. The first three hitters bang out singles, and he gets taken out. Well, guess what? From the 7th inning on, opponents are now hitting an elite .333 against him (3 for 9 over those three appearances).

He makes his next start. He's rolling again. He looks the way he did the first two starts. After the 6th inning is done, the manager looks at his chart. "Oh, they're batting .333 against him from the 7th inning on. Better take him out without even talking to him."

That's overuse. That's overmanaging. Ignoring the fact that what a guy does the first six innings in one game is independent of what he's doing in the next game. This is why you have to watch. This is why you can't just plug in a few calculations and never get out of bed. This oversimplified strategy of assuming everyone will either progress or regress to their means is not congruent with what actually happens on a day-by-day basis. But the analytics thinkers still insist that analytics is the last piece to the puzzle in solving the mystery of baseball. Well it isn't. Some degree of mystery will remain, no matter what analytics ever produces, and its overuse has only opened the door to one-track-minded laziness. Overusing analytics is like giving an answer to a misunderstood question. It's like asking me what my favorite color is, and I say, "Riding a bicycle."

DISCRETION

It's, of course, impossible to always perfectly time when you should pull your starter. You're always going to disagree with the manager sometimes, and fans will never know what's going on inside the dugout or why. However, at whatever point a starter appears on his way down, the manager should go out and *talk to him* before he does anything else. Take his temperature, so to speak. We all know the starter will want to stay in, but this is where the manager's actual job comes into play. He must know his players and whether or how much more he can push them. It takes savvy discretion to do this, and savvy discretion occurs intuitively.

OZZIE GUILLEN

Due to his outstanding discretion, this former White Sox manager is responsible for the best-managed postseason in recent years. En route to the 2005 White Sox's 11-1 October and first championship in eighty-eight years, Guillen's starters pitched 92 innings in 12 games. Averaging 7.2 innings per start, the starter began the 9th inning in five of those 12 games. In the American League Championship Series (ALCS), Guillen's winning starters went the distance in Games 2, 3, 4, and 5! Guillen never obsessed with pitch count or making sure his relievers got in, and he didn't fall in love with his rookie smoke-throwing closer, Bobby Jenks. At his best discretion,

Guillen just let his starters work for the duration that they were effective. And when the bullpen was needed, they were more able to deliver because they weren't overused. The White Sox bullpen pitched 11.2 innings before giving up a run, and they only allowed three runs in 21 innings.

Today's managers would have gone gaga if their bullpen was doing that well. Rather than consider that maybe the bullpen was excelling because their workload wasn't overly demanding, they would have overmanaged and built every game around them. Had Guillen done the same thing, maybe the White Sox wouldn't have gone all the way.

You bring in your closer (or any reliever, for that matter) when the game is getting tight—*not* when only a five-run homer can tie the game. After airing him out in Game 5, it was ludicrous beyond description that Maddon would even think of bringing in Chapman to finish the 7th inning of Game 6. But why stop there? Then Chapman pitched the 8th, and then Maddon let him walk the leadoff hitter in the 9th inning with what was now a seven-run lead before finally replacing him. Chapman only threw 20 pitches in Game 6, but that's a lot, having just thrown 42 in the eight-and-a-half-month-long season's final week two days prior.

After that 9th inning walk, I wondered...what was Maddon going to do if Chapman *did* retire the first hitter? Was he just going to stay with him until someone reached base?

Maddon needed to do anything to finish Game 6 without Chapman, and it wasn't that long ago managers would have done precisely that. Maddon needed to realize if Chapman didn't rest in Game 6, then things were likelier to get precarious in Game 7. Maddon obviously couldn't afford to let things get *too* tight, but not only did he not make even the slightest effort to avoid Chapman, he also tried to make him do the entire bullpen's job. And the Cubs are so lucky they weren't horribly screwed the next day, like they very easily could have been.

As I'm constantly ripping the managers, I am aware of the unspoken understanding that the manager isn't the manager anymore. Many of today's preplanned decisions are assembled by the front office, and the guy referred to as the manager silently carries them out, regardless of whether he agrees. At this point, the front office and manager should just be called the managing staff. That is a total sham in and of itself, and Bill Madlock concurred, adding that many in-game decisions are so poor that there's no way they could have come from a baseball mind.

GAME 7

The Cubs are touching up Corey Kluber, and Kyle Hendricks is pitching. Hendricks had a great season for Chicago, and tonight was going no different. In a rhythm. Getting ahead in the count with first pitch curveballs consistently. Hendricks had one stressful inning early on but had been coasting ever since. Then…

A two-out walk to Carlos Santana in the bottom of the 5th. Instant hook! Get Hendricks's 5–1 lead and his 63 pitches out of there! 63! 63? Yup. The *Titanic* has split into two and is sinking fast. Not that he should have, but former closer Keith Foulke once threw 59 pitches in the 9th to finish a game. Yet Kyle Hendricks, who'd had a Cy Young--caliber season, was yanked before completing even five smooth innings in Game 7 of the World Series. In just a couple of seasons, baseball went from not letting the starter throw more than X number of pitches to removing him when he reaches a specific point of the game. Thanks to analytics' overuse, even pitch count has become irrelevant.

On Opening Day of 2018, the Phillies' rookie manager Gabe Kapler pulled Aaron Nola in the 6th inning. Nola had only thrown 68 pitches and was cruising. The bullpen got bombed, and the Phillies lost. The fans already wanted Kapler fired. After one game!

Obviously, anyone can sit here and criticize decisions, but that's not what this is about. I'm just highlighting the heaviest, most vile extremes overusing analytics has gone to. When Nola was taken out, he stood on the mound in disbelief. Just because you have three frying pans doesn't mean you must use all three when scrambling three eggs. Just because you have a bullpen full of relievers doesn't mean you have to use them. They're only there if you need them. They're called *relief* pitchers. They are there to provide *relief*.

Even Trump chimed in on how disgraceful baseball now is. During Game 4 of the 2018 World Series, he tweeted: "Watching the Dodgers/Red Sox final innings. It is amazing how a manager takes out a pitcher who is loose and dominating through almost 7 innings. Rich Hill of Dodgers, and brings in nervous reliever(s) who get shellacked. 4 run lead gone. Managers do it all the time, big mistake!"

When Trump is out of office, maybe his next walk of life will be managing baseball. Going off that tweet, I'd say he's already more qualified than most, if not all of today's managing staffs. I didn't ask Bill Madlock about Trump, but he did express that you can't do any worse than plenty of today's managers, and part of the reason is that they don't have to work their way up anymore—someone who has done nothing managerially can still get hired as long as they're willing to go along with the front office and not say who makes what decisions.

But all right. Hendricks was done as the Cubs went to the big-money veteran Jon Lester. Lester started Game 5, throwing 90 pitches in six innings. Given how unusual of a task this was, the potential long-relief outing Lester was about to make on only two days rest was a risky maneuver. What would have been minimally risky was Kyle Hendricks continuing to pitch because he pitched at least five innings in all 30 of his regular-season starts, and at least six innings in 20 of them.

WHAT HAS HAPPENED TO BASEBALL?

When sizing up the sensibility of a decision, it never matters how things turn out because you can only go on what's in front of you at the time the decision is made. You cannot be results oriented, and that is something poker players always remind themselves of. Hitting some long-shot card to win a big pot doesn't mean you made a good decision because you didn't know you were going to catch such a break. The same thing goes when you lose a big pot. You might have misplayed your hand, but maybe you did everything perfectly and just got unlucky.

If the Angels trade Mike Trout to the Padres for a turkey sandwich, it's a terrible trade for the Angels because Mike Trout adds more value to a baseball team than one turkey sandwich will. I know that because I did the analytics. So it doesn't matter if Mike Trout suddenly decides he'd rather open a chain of popcorn stands and forgoes every dollar of his contract, or if the turkey sandwich turns out to have fairy dust in it and makes every Angel play like an All-Star.

It's true that an apparent nincompoop-looking decision may have included some shrewd foresight by the decision maker, but I guarantee you that was not the case when Maddon pulled Hendricks. It was an automatic, preplanned decision to go to Jon Lester if someone reached base in the 5th inning, and none of the Cubs' managing staff cared that their great starting pitcher was once again looking great.

Lester got unlucky at first. A swinging bunt led to runners being on second and third base instead of first and second, and then a wild pitch led to two runs scoring instead of one. It was a pretty zany back-to-back sequence of events. But what's that expression? You make your own luck? It served the managing staff right to have to stomach that after taking out Hendricks.

After that, Lester cooled everything down and settled into a beautiful rhythm just like Hendricks. This doesn't mean bringing Lester in was wise, because again, you cannot be results oriented. Since there was no sensible reason whatsoever for removing Hendricks to begin with, I don't give Maddon or anybody on the managing staff credit for going to Lester.

The Cubs took a 6–3 lead into the bottom of the 8th, and the taste of victory was getting very real. The Indians had two out and nobody on, but this was the calm before the storm. Jon Lester completely, and I mean *completely*, imploded. He gave up an infield single to José Ramirez.

For a second time in this Game 7, Joe Maddon immediately took the ball from a prevailing pitcher because someone innocently reached first base with two outs. And in came Aroldis Chapman.

Overworked and faultlessly unable to accurately locate his pitches, Chapman was greeted by a ringing run-scoring double by Brandon Guyer, and then a sensationally stunning game-tying two-run homer by Rajai Davis, who had hit just 55 career home runs in 3,687 at-bats—it was the first home run Chapman had allowed in 210 batters. Coco Crisp followed with a sharp single, and Chapman finally ended the batting practice session by striking out Yan Gomes and his paltry .201 OBP.

I was watching the game with a friend who bet heavily on the Indians to win Game 7 (I'd also bet the Indians to win the series, but I'd bet before Game 1). After the Cubs didn't score in the top of the 9th, I turned to him and said, "Well, I'll promise you one thing. There is no way they are bringing Chapman back out for the 9th."

Sure enough, when the action returned, there Chapman was. Why? Because he's the closer, the ace reliever. Analytics says, "Forget how good Jon Lester looked, and forget how gassed Aroldis Chapman obviously is." The certainty of analytics' intellect has declared him to be the optimal choice, so he's getting the ball.

Out of all the astonishing things I'd seen to that point in my first 31.6 years of consciousness, this was the pinnacle moment of my existence. Seeing Aroldis Chapman handed the ball to pitch the bottom of this 9th inning after getting tattooed in the 8th was the single-most beside-myself moment I'd ever felt. "What the *hell* am I looking at right now and how much longer do I wait before I commit myself? I have to be hallucinating. I have to be! There is simply no way I am actually seeing what I am seeing, because it is just that maniacal."

Here comes the 3-2 pitch to Carlos Santana leading off. It's a hanging slider, and he flies out to shallow left field.

"Ohhhh my God!" I screamed. "That was it!!! That could have been it right there!"

But that's baseball, you know? That's sports, and that's why we watch. Aroldis Chapman started going to his slider because he couldn't locate his fastball—he hung another slider to Jason Kipnis but survived with a 1-2-3 inning. The Cubs went ahead 8-6 in the 10th, and Carl Edwards Jr. and Mike Montgomery held on for dear life to secure the 8-7 championship victory.

I give all the credit to the Cubs and none to the managing staff. I don't care how they built such a great team using analytics because in the end, they were lucky they didn't tear everything down exactly the way they built it. Getting to Game 7 of the World Series is a major accomplishment, but I don't think losing it is what Cubs fans had in mind.

Hindsight being twenty-twenty, it's easy to say Chapman should have been left in because of his scoreless 9th inning. But no one did! It went without saying that letting him continue was nothing shy of a death wish. If a starting pitcher goes five innings and gives up four earned runs, then he had to have thrown up at least one goose egg. With everything being equal, giving up four earned runs in five innings is terrible. Just because you tossed a scoreless inning doesn't mean you were any good. Scoring runs is hard.

It was nothing short of a miracle that both Santana and Kipnis didn't crush those hanging sliders over 400 feet. It was a miracle Chapman got through the 9th inning at all, and the most bewildering part of this miracle is Chapman set down Cleveland's top of the order in Santana, Kipnis, and Francisco Lindor.

Stolen signs or not, there was no miracle for Chapman's hanging slider three years later when José Altuve homered off him in Game 6 to walk-off the 2019 ALCS. But the life experience itself is a miracle. And in Game 7 of the 2016 World Series, the baseball gods *finally* decided, "Okay, enough is enough is enough. Tonight, we stop farting in the mouths of Cubs fans. Because if we don't, they will behead Joe Maddon and carry his skull on a pike along Waveland Avenue."

I sincerely believe that's why the Cubs won Game 7. If it's not, it sure wasn't because of analytics.

4TH INNING:
STRIKEOUTS, HOME RUNS, AND WALKS

These three occurrences have taken over baseball because they are "true outcomes," meaning that they occur without any variables. Nothing else could have happened in their place. Something like a hitter grounding a single into left field is not considered a true outcome because something else might have happened to get him out.

STRIKE EVERYBODY OUT

The crafty pitcher who pitches to contact by effectively changing speeds and location has become obsolete because analytics thinkers have concluded there's too much luck involved once the ball is put in play. The strikeout has become the most desired outcome, because what can go wrong? If the hitter makes contact, he might get on base. If he doesn't, he can't. It's black and white.

It's true there's always a possibility of good or bad luck any time the ball is hit, but pitchers have been turning in dominant performances by pitching to contact since baseball began. So this idea that there's suddenly all this luck involved whenever the ball is put in play is unwelcome—that is a most outlandish exaggeration. Keeping hitters off balance by pitching to weak contact isn't luck. It takes savvy strategy and precise skill. Not to mention that because of analytics, pitchers are surrendering fewer hits—teams adjust their defensive alignment based on who's hitting. How fitting that analytics says to rack up strikeouts, yet analytics is also why doing so has become less necessary.

Whenever you go for the jugular at something, opposite the reward, there is a large risk. If a fighter goes for a knockout, he is likelier to get knocked out. If a defensive back goes for an interception, the receiver is likelier to score a touchdown. If a poker player tries to bluff, he is likelier to lose a big pot. If a fisherman tries to catch a great white shark, he is likelier to be eaten alive. If a hitter tries to hit a home run, he is likelier to be retired. And if a pitcher tries to strike a hitter out, he is likelier to surrender a home run.

When pitching to contact, yes, you leave the door open to things like broken-bat hits, parachute doubles, swinging bunts, seeing-eye singles, errors, and other annoying things, but there's going to be a cost, no matter which approach you take.

I have nothing against power pitching specifically. However, there are only so many guys who are maximally effective in throwing smoke *and* who can do it every year without incurring permanent damage. Bill Madlock said he's never seen so many injured pitchers, and it's because they're all groomed to throw hard.

In today's game, most starting pitchers know they won't pitch past the 6th inning, and this allows their state of mind to more easily settle into fastball-sprint mode. However, since most pitchers are not built to blow everyone away, it's a mistake to make their body learn something it isn't built for.

The skills athletes should hone the most are the ones that came naturally. Let them get great at what they are already good at. Forcing something that is unnatural harms their athletic intelligence and ability to perform intuitively. Just let players be themselves, and *that's* how their contributions will be maximized.

Analytics doesn't know what team unity is, but a team can unite when everyone knows all of their teammates are unselfishly focused on delivering their top skills. When players are being who and what they are, that energy ripples throughout the team. So assembling a good pitching staff is not as simple as collecting the most guys who can throw 98 mph. Analytics thinkers just think that because the computer doesn't watch the game or go in the clubhouse. I also don't go in the clubhouse, but this is my understanding as to how team chemistry works.

Trying to strike everyone out in Little League is a good idea, but it's unnecessary at the show because the fielders can actually field. By letting your defense defend, you expend less energy in two ways. One, you throw fewer pitches, and two, you burn yourself out less per pitch because you're not constantly throwing smoke. This allows you to pitch longer before needing the bench pitchers, and you'll also be more effective when you do have to bear down for a strikeout (like when there's a runner on third base with fewer than two outs) because you haven't been doing it the whole game. And unlike the crafty pitcher who can get you out multiple ways, the fireballer has a minimal shot at salvaging a respectable outing on a day he's wild or doesn't have his good fastball.

By insisting on one strategy, you also give the hitters the whole game to adjust. This leaves you with minimal elements of surprise or unfamiliarity. That's why Bill Madlock tells his up-and-coming hitters to look for fastballs. As pitchers are very cocky in their heaters, their main concern is lighting up the radar gun. But it doesn't matter how hard they throw because hitters can catch up to anything made easy for them to time. Madlock said you can get a hitter out throwing 60 mph. He (and everyone else who has made statements comparable to that) is right because a savvy pitcher can gas you throwing just 88 mph. If a hitter is fooled by the speed, then what chance does he really have? Not to mention that the more pitchers who throw 98 mph, the less exceptional it is. Yet every time a new flamethrower enters, the announcers say, "Ohhh, this guy hits 98 consistently on the gun!"

Recording strikeouts was and still is supposed to be situationally dependent. A strikeout's value depends on the quality of its timing, not its overall quantity. If you can't get a strikeout when in a jam, then your other strikeouts are accomplishing the minimum. That's why the most tolerant I am of a hitter striking out is when the bases are empty. The greater the rally, the less tolerant I am. This is all completely congruent with pitching. Strikeouts are great, but I only need them when they'll directly keep runs off the board.

I would like to see pitchers again be groomed to pitch however they do most effortlessly and be taught how to strategize deceptively, no matter how hard they throw—because no matter what stats analytics thinkers can present, good pitching still revolves around the same principles. It's mainly about conserving your energy when things are tame, and then bearing down when in trouble. Today's pitchers essentially bear down the whole game. Then, when they really need to, the difference in how much they can is much smaller.

HOME RUNS, HOME RUNS, AND MORE HOME RUNS

Baseball has been oversimply reduced to power pitching and power hitting. Once upon a time, it was rare to see a guy consistently throw 98 mph. Once upon a time, it was embarrassing for a hitter to strike out (Bill Madlock said if he had ever struck out 100 times in a season, he would have probably shot himself). Once upon a time, it was relatively likely to see a game without any home runs. Once upon a time, baseball was dynamic.

There is an enormous contradiction going on between the strikeout and home run. Pitchers are told to always go for strikeouts because they're invaluable, but hitters are told striking out is okay. This is incapable of making sense. A strikeout can *only* be as great for the pitcher as it is bad for the hitter. If it's no big deal for a hitter to strike out, then it's no big deal for the pitcher to strike him out. How can a pitcher recording a strikeout be 10/10 in terms of value if it's not a 10/10 disaster for the hitter?

The other end of the contradiction is that hitters are told to swing for the fences. Never mind the score, never mind the count, never mind the inning, never mind how the pitcher is doing, never mind what kind of pitcher he is, never mind how you might be pitched to in this particular AB, never mind how you're doing so far in this particular AB, never mind which way the wind might be blowing, never mind *anything*. Just try to park one because homering is the best thing you can do. Yet pitchers are told, "Don't stress solo home runs. The homers to prevent are those with at least one baserunner." Once again, this cannot make sense. If it's no big deal for a pitcher to a surrender a solo home run, then hitting one can only be so valuable for the hitter.

Hitters aren't just taught to swing for the downs once they're strong enough to clear the fence. Now they're groomed to learn home-run-hitting techniques right from the beginning. Bill Madlock talked about witnessing five-year-old kids being taught to swing straight up in the air to achieve a proper launch angle. I wasn't surprised to hear that, but it still made me a little sick.

We hardly ever see a hitter survey the field anymore when he steps into the box. You know, look around and see who's playing where. There are far fewer adjustments to the situation (even though everyone constantly talks about how important adjusting is) because baseball players are now taught, "Don't worry about the other stuff. Just try to hit home runs because if you can just hit one every six games, you'll have a job."

Bill Madlock said the worst hitters he's ever seen are all playing today. He talked about what we see all the time: teams get runners on second and/or third base and don't even come close to scoring. Hitters swing as hard as possible, no matter what the count is. Anthony Rizzo is known for choking up with two strikes, but besides him, nobody ever backs off their swing to try and make hard contact somewhere else. And what really drives Madlock (and me) nuts is hearing announcers ramble on about guys who have 20 home runs and 50 RBIs like they're superstars.

Home runs are given so much acclaim now that when you see the scores running across the bottom of the screen on ESPN, they tell you a home run's distance when it's a moon shot—as if home runs are especially important when they happen to be 450-foot prodigious blasts. This sends the message that baseball is about home runs: hit them as far as possible as often as possible because it's cool.

Now that Commissioner Rob Manfred admitted something needs to be done about the apparently juiced baseball, it's currently inaccurate to keeping calling baseball "baseball."

"Bombball" is run by people who have thought, "Well, home runs sell. But steroids are out, so what can we do instead? Ah! Let's juice the ball. We'll make the seams thinner. This will lessen air resistance, allowing the ball to fly out of the park more easily."

It was nice of Manfred to come out and say it, but it's not like we needed anyone to tell us the ball is different. Forget about launch angle and what players are taught. When *this* many players suddenly have a staggering increase in their home run total *and* the consistent long distance they were traveling, something is up. There were 450-plus-foot blasts practically every day in 2019, not to mention that one medium-deep fly ball after another had a way of going and going and going. Outfielders, announcers, myself, and many fans were routinely fooled by lazy fly balls that somehow ended up twenty feet behind the fence.

In discussing how to design a winning bombball team, one former executive said, "The team that hits more home runs than the opposition usually wins."

It doesn't matter if this statement is correct because winning does not boil down to outhomering your opponent. That is so oversimplified. If your primary concern is hitting home runs, you become an all-or-nothing and predictable team. You're the same as the pitcher who constantly airs out his fastball. Your strategy is completely transparent, leaving yourself with nothing to do when adjusted to or in a team funk. You are not dynamic because you lack balance. And as a side effect, you probably have more below-average fielders because power hitters have always gotten more leeway on their defense.

Just like flamethrowers are going to rack up some extra strikeouts for show, I know sluggers are going to hit some insignificant home runs. You can't always tie the game, take the lead, get back in a game, or put a game away. But like strikeouts, a home run's value is situationally dependent. It's about the quality, not the quantity.

I get really annoyed when I see a 9th inning solo home run make a 5–0 game 5–1. It's like, What were you doing? Did you try to hit a home run, or are you just that good of a hitter? When trailing in the 9th inning, home runs are only extra valuable if they can tie or win the game. I can't stand when I hear fans cheering loudly for a 9th inning home run that only made the score closer because a bunt single would have been just as productive. Home runs clear the bases, so that does limit the ways the defense can record outs, but this small reward is not worth the risk needed to try and crank one. The 9th inning is your last offensive possession, so first things first—you need baserunners to bring up the tying run.

Just as you should only be looking to strike someone out when in a jam, you should only be looking downtown when a pitcher is tiring or when it's going to change the game. Since solo homers aren't taken as a big deal for the pitcher to surrender, then don't go out of your way to hit them unless it's going to be a game changer. Look to average more RBIs per home run rather than pile up home runs that average fewer RBIs per home run.

Overemphasizing hitting home runs or recording strikeouts is no different than a poker player who bluffs too much. It's not a mistake to be aggressive. In what game does success not highly predicate on aggression? Aggression is great—until it's all you're doing. It puts you out of balance, so you have to play conservatively sometimes to maximize your aggression's effectiveness. If you don't, you become predictably exploitable. The same thing goes if you're too conservative. Patience is magnificent, but you become transparent if you're only aggressive when you have a strong hand.

Like with strikeouts, the huge spike in home runs makes each home run less valuable than the last one. Home runs don't seem like an exciting achievement anymore because they occur so often. But the biggest problem with the obsession of home runs and strikeouts is that no one is exploiting it. Bombball is being played well below its highest possible level. America's pastime went from being very technical to throwing nothing but haymakers. It would be like if ten people competing in a 100-meter dash all decided to run zigzags instead of straight lines. No one's inefficiency is being exploited because everyone is doing it, so the overall quality suffers.

Poker's quality has never been a present-day joke because, unlike bombball, poker has never gone backward since it started going forward. I'm a much better player now than I was ten years ago, but I was a more dominant player back then because the field was weaker. The top players from at least a decade ago made so many mistakes so routinely, it's unbelievable. They were essentially trying to strike everyone out and hit home runs, but they didn't get exploited that much because no one knew how or why they could. They really weren't mistakes in that regard since it was all relative, but it's not relative with bombball. How to exploit all the stupidity *is* known. It's just that no one will do it.

THERE IS NO CLOCK!

The most gaping difference between baseball and the other sports is you *have* to fail. You are required to do what the opposition wants. You must make 27 outs (possibly 24 when leading at home) to complete your win. In the NFL, you don't have to fumble. In the NBA, you don't have to miss a shot. In the UFC, you don't have to get elbowed in the face. But in baseball, you have to make outs. Finishing the game *predicates* on you failing.

Since it is mandatory to fail at least 24 times, doesn't it make sense to at least try to get the most production out of each out? Especially when you consider you could go 162-0 with a team batting average of .000?

Suppose it's the 1st inning with a runner on third base and one out. The infield is playing back, so a routine ground ball to the second baseman or shortstop will bring in a run, as will a fly ball that is relatively deep. A strikeout does nothing but prevent the next guy from driving in a run with an out.

I'm actually amazed I felt the need to write that. That's how far out of proportion analytics is used. I'm not saying you should always give yourself up when in the above situation. I'm saying that like poker, every situation can call for a different strategy. Sometimes you should swing for the fences, sometimes you should look for a single, and sometimes you should make sure to advance the lead runner. One thing you must never allow is yourself to be unaware of how costly striking out will be.

It's as though baseball needs to be dumbed down completely, so let's just start with this: hit the damn ball, and something good might happen!

THE WALK

Whenever I read up on players' careers during the '90s, I always looked at their OBP and walk totals. It's surprising that only in the last decade or two did we finally start to hear about the importance of walks and OBP. Drawing walks are now incredibly vital in today's game, but how much value do they really provide?

I'm hardly denying that walks are *huge*. Issuing walks is brutal for the pitcher, so that means it's great for the hitter. A pitcher's wildness drives up his pitch count. This makes a pitcher feel an urge to throw a strike, and this makes him more liable to throw you a cookie. Walks are foolproof production—hence the true outcome label they've been given. Despite this, walks have still gone from being undervalued to overvalued.

When's the last time you heard an announcer talk about a game that was busted open with a walk? You haven't because walks are the setup. They're like the jab. You can knock someone out with a jab, but it's pretty hard. The walk is a critical supplement that you can't expect to win without, but a hit can drive in a baserunner from any base depending on where and how it lands. When you draw a walk, the most that can happen is every runner moves up one base. And in many cases, no runners advance or only one runner advances.

Despite the lovely saying, a walk is not as good as a hit. Hits are more efficient, and errors can occur whenever the ball is hit. If hits weren't more efficient and threatening than walks, then there would never be an intentional walk. There's an incurred risk to issuing an IBB because you're adding another baserunner, but it sets up a more desirable pitching matchup and always a double-play possibility.

Perhaps the easiest proof that walks are overrated is the great Joey Votto, who has taken criticism for walking too much with runners on base. If walks are so important, then you can't give a guy with one of the highest career OBPs a hard time. You'd think I'd agree with this criticism, but I don't, because I can't fault a hitter for taking a ball—trying to own RBIs can get a hitter into bad habits. However, if that hitter can somehow develop an ability to turn strike zone expansion on and off when appropriate, then all the better.

Which .800 OPS player would you rather have up in the 9th inning with the bases loaded, two outs, and trailing by two runs? A .250 hitter with a .375 OBP, or a .300 hitter with a .344 OBP? It's a bit of a vague and open-ended question, but I lean toward the .300 hitter.

It isn't black and white that the guy with the higher OBP should always be preferred because there are situations where you have to get a *hit*. A walk won't be enough. Looking to draw one will either be too unlikely to happen, or it'll just leave it up to the next guy. At critical junctures, I want someone dynamic. Someone who can have a tough AB with or without a great OBP. Someone who can hit a good pitch because batting .300 is exceptional. A .250 hitter is primarily a mistake hitter, and this is not reliable. Analytics thinkers have very foolishly concluded that batting average isn't that important. I agree it's less important than it was once considered, but now the pendulum has swung to the other extreme.

An example of a very valuable player without an exceptional OBP was José Reyes. Reyes drew only enough walks to maintain a respectable OBP, but what made him valuable was his power and speed. For seven seasons with the Mets and Marlins, he averaged 52 stolen bases (with a very high success rate of 79.2 percent), 58 extra base hits, and a .345 OBP. Reyes got into scoring position seemingly every time he reached base. He was often, at most, a routine single away from being knocked in. This is a rarely provided luxury, especially when you consider how many times Reyes crossed from second base to third base on a ground ball to the third baseman.

If you get on base with a .375 clip but have limited speed and power, it will often take a lot more for you to score than it would for someone like Reyes. The .375 OBP is great, but it doesn't tell you the whole story. That's why we have OPS. OPS's calculation doesn't factor in stolen bases, but it magnifies how you're getting on base in addition to how often.

THE OAKLAND ATHLETICS

People often say what a crapshoot the MLB postseason is, and to some extent, they are. One five-game series and two seven-game series are nothing compared to the 162-game season. A longer postseason would be that much more revealing, but as it is, I still think the cream tends to rise to the top. As much as I hate to admit it, the best team I ever saw was the Yankees when they won four rings in five seasons from 1996 to 2000. That group knew how to win, and it wasn't because they could set dice.

Since the Oakland Athletics made this whole analytics and sabermetrics thing famous, let's look at how it's worked out for them so far:

As of 2000, Oakland has done very well. If they went about their business besides the way they have, they probably would have far less success since they can't compete financially. The A's have made the postseason seven times (ten times if you dare include their wildcard game losses in 2014, 2018, and 2019). They lost in the American League Division Series (ALDS) opening round six times. They lost the decisive Game 5 in all six, five of which were in Oakland. The one time they reached the ALCS in 2006, the Tigers swept them in four.

In the 1,133 games played during those seven regular seasons, Oakland averaged 1.21 home runs, 3.82 walks, and 4.99 runs per game with a .257 team batting average. In their 37 postseason games, they averaged

0.86 home runs (down 29 percent), 3 walks (down 21 percent), and 3.51 runs per game (down 30 percent) with a .237 team batting average (down 8 percent).

Maybe this should all remind us that hitting home runs and drawing walks isn't enough to become a champion—you need other ways to score. If you don't have them, then your results become far more luck dependent because your approach is inflexible. You need guys who can hit all over the field and guys who can wreak havoc on the bases. They don't have to steal that many bases, but they need to at least pose the threat. Analytics can't measure distractions. How much a rabbit on first base affects a pitcher's concentration is not quantifiable, but it definitely has an impact because keeping a runner from getting into scoring position is critical.

I know some people will play the crapshoot "small sample size" card all day in defending the A's, but I'm not having it. This wasn't just 37 games. This was 37 postseason games showing us just how far sabermetrics will get you. It's fun hitting a bunch of home runs and running up the score against bad pitching during the long regular season, but that doesn't mean you are a good *team*. Bill Madlock agreed the home-run barrage can get you to October, but it's likely to fail in the postseason's short series because now you're consistently facing good pitching. The challenge will become too great, as you now have to get astronomically lucky to do any significant damage.

Through all the drastic new points of view that have completely changed baseball, three very simple things haven't changed: a winning baseball team needs great starting pitching, a sure-handed defense, and timely hitting. No one knew winning baseball was about these things *before* they started playing. They discovered it intuitively like anything else! Just like the first poker players saw that as emotions fly as much as the money, emotions are advantageously readable through intuition.

These basic principles to baseball and poker will never be false, no matter how much analytics and GTO helps deepen our technical understanding of each game. You can't just scrap something's roots because you developed some cool formulas. Analytics and GTO are only meant to *add* to their game's key elements. They should not *replace* them. That is overestimating their value, and that is exactly what baseball has been doing.

A quality-run baseball team will have executives who can sense what's missing. Using logic and illogic, they can figure out what combination of players is most likely to dynamically gel in the clubhouse and on the field. If you insist winning is as easy as piling up flamethrowers and home-run hitters who walk because all three are true outcomes, well, good luck. You'll be needing it.

5ᵀᴴ INNING:
PROPOSED CHANGES

Major League Baseball has quite a few head-scratching rules and nonrules that are easily correctable. Some have been there awhile, some have been recently implemented, and there are some I want to see implemented.

ELIMINATE ALL POSSIBILITIES FOR FAN INTERFERENCE

The fact that the rulebook has a section on "fan interference" is already a farce. Fan interference? What the hell is that? Why would the *fans* ever be even remotely capable of interfering with anything? Fans are there to watch, cheer, eat, goof on their phones, and possibly drink. That's it! At no point should a fan ever come anywhere close to getting involved with a play. If you're not allowed to touch the food samples inside the glass case at a Starbucks, why would you be allowed to interfere with a Major League Baseball game?

I have been bugging out for years over the fact that fans get to sit right on top of the action. Going up and down the left and right field lines, fans seated in the front row reach across the railing *onto the playing field*. They disrupt fielders from making plays, and they snatch fair balls, causing ground rule doubles. Sometimes when reaching over the railing, fans fall on the field! Have you ever asked yourself, "What is a fan doing on the field?"

Fans sit inches behind the home-run wall too. Some stadiums don't have seats behind the outfield fences, but that's not enough. There needs to be space between the fans and the players all over every part of every stadium—just a simple gap of several feet so that there will never be a stupid, inexplicable, avoidable, and controversial fan interference fiasco ever again.

Imagine this football scenario:

"Mahomes takes the snap, he drops back, rolls left, looking, looking, he's got a man down the sidelines, and…ohhhh, and a fan reaches in and breaks up the pass! We'll have to go to video review now to see if there was fan interference preventing the receiver from making the catch."

If fans sat on the sidelines during a football game, or a basketball game, or a soccer game, or any freakin' game, it'd be no different from what baseball has been allowing this whole time.

I'm really not trying to be the grinch who stole baseball. I know sports are for the fans—but not to participate. That is why the fans do not get paid, and that is why there is nothing unwelcoming about pushing them back *a few feet*. As it is, it's like letting the audience sit on the stage at a Cirque du Soleil show.

Maybe Major League Baseball is afraid to do this because anything the fans might perceive as unfriendly could make profits decrease. Whatever the reason why we never hear a peep about this, the question is: Where do you draw the line? At what point do you stop compromising baseball's integrity? I don't care that fans get kicked out for interfering because they shouldn't have the opportunity to begin with! MLB tolerating this does not make baseball more unique, or more personal, or more anything. It's just plain dumb.

WHAT HAS HAPPENED TO BASEBALL?

It happened:

Game 1 of the 1996 ALCS. Orioles at Yankees. It's the bottom of the 8th inning, and the Yankees are down 4–3. In comes the young fireballer Armando Benitez. Derek Jeter is up. With one out, Jeter skies one to deep right field. It's carrying, but Tony Tarasco has a beat on it. He camps under it. He's waiting to put it away for the F-9…oops! Jeffrey Maier, a twelve-year-old child, sticks his glove over the fence and snatches it away. Instead of being the second out, the Yankees tied the game because a fan prevented the Major League Baseball player from catching the baseball.

More than two decades later, all everyone still talks about is how bad of a missed call it was. The umpire did make an unacceptably egregious mistake, but *that is not the point!* And since the umpire was that close to the play and still managed to botch it up, it only makes it more imperative that there not be seats right behind the fence.

The Orioles went on to lose Game 1 in extra innings. They won Game 2, but then lost all three games in Baltimore and were sent home. We have no way of knowing what would have happened had Jeter's "home run" been recorded as the out it 100 percent should have been, but that play may very well have affected the outcome of the entire 1996 postseason—not because the umpire should have ruled it an out; Tarasco just should have been able to do his job *uninhibited*.

I realize that to be a champion, you have to withstand adversity, but no team should have to overcome something like that. These players work too hard and make too much money to have to worry about fans interfering. This happens nowhere else in sports, but for some reason, MLB lacks the brains or the guts to do something that is very simple: *take the fans out of the equation.*

It happened:

October again. Game 4 of the 2018 ALCS. Red Sox at Astros. The Red Sox lead the series 2-1, and the Astros are batting in the bottom of the 1st. The Astros trail 2-0 and have a runner on first with one out. José Altuve drives one deep to right field. The Gold Glover Mookie Betts goes back and perfectly times a *stupendous* athletic leap into the stands! But some fans pushed Betts's glove closed before he could possibly rob Altuve's possible home run.

Initially, the ball was ruled in play. The lead runner was held at third base, and Altuve made it to second. During the video replay, it appeared Betts was right in line to make the catch. But who could say for sure? The announcers talked about what a tough call it was. *Yes!* That's why this can't be a possibility! Having the fans sit there not only leads to delays but it also makes these close and gigantic calls extremely difficult to make.

The worst part about this utter nonsense is it thoroughly ruins the exquisiteness of what we could have watched—what we're *paying* to watch. Instead of getting to see Mookie Betts make a marvelous attempt to rob a home run *in a postseason game*, we have to stop the game and see if the random people who have nothing, absolutely *nothing*, to do with anything, interfered. Unbelievable.

They ended up ruling Altuve out for fan interference, and the lead runner was sent back to first base. I agreed with the ruling, but it was so anticlimactic because the thrill of the moment was long gone.

I don't care if it's the postseason or spring training. Fans are only supposed to watch. So, until baseball players start coming by people's desks to interfere with their work, no one will convince me preventing fans from interfering is "taking" something from them.

It happened:

Regular season, 2018. Mets at Dodgers. During the middle innings, Alex Verdugo hits a pop fly foul ball, and Mets third baseman Todd Frazier is in hot pursuit. Running toward the stands, he reaches out, catches the ball, and then tumbles into the first row of seats.

To confirm the out, Frazier showed the ball to the umpire, who was right on top of the play. FF-5 on your scorecard. Great catch! Highlight worthy. Or was it?

The next day, replay revealed that Todd Frazier did not catch the ball—he lost it as he fell. Not a surprise, considering his body was all contorted and crowded among a bunch of fans and seats. *But* while his body was sprawled out, Frazier noticed another baseball in close proximity—a plaything piece of rubber that belonged to a kid. Frazier picked it up, showed the umpire, received credit for the out, and then tossed it into the stands to show what a nice guy he is. Video replay also showed a fan holding the actual baseball.

Is this a joke? I'm afraid not. Todd Frazier's dishonesty in picking up a phony baseball and presenting it to get an out is hysterical, but this is no laughing matter. Not only did Todd Frazier steal an out by sneakily showing a fan's baseball (possibly a purchased souvenir?), it wasn't even a real baseball. It was a toy. The Mets recorded an out because their third baseman gained access to an opposing fan's toy. What a circus. An absolute travesty.

Major League Baseball: *wake up*. You cannot have dropped foul balls turn into outs because a fielder managed to (without permission) borrow someone else's fake baseball.

It happened:

Regular season, early 1990s. Yankee Stadium. There's a pop fly foul ball off to the right. Yankee first baseman Don Mattingly goes over for a look, but it's well into the crowd. As he looked, a small boy who was also following the play was snacking on a bag of popcorn. With the boy's head turned, Mattingly reached into the kid's bag and snatched a few kernels.

It was hilarious, but that great moment is not worth all the disasters that can and frequently do happen. I just want to see the baseball players play baseball. I would like to see the players affect the entire outcome. Is that so much to ask?

It happened:

I couldn't remember all the details well enough to find the video, but I think the Yankees were playing the Red Sox in Boston. In any event, I vividly remember someone doubling down the right field line. Yankee right-fielder Gary Sheffield went over to the side wall, and threw the ball back in. Except before doing so (and this is bizarrely humorous in its own right), Sheffield pushed a fan sitting in the front row. Why? Well, as Sheffield was picking up the ball, a fan stuck his arm out. He didn't lunge at Sheffield or do anything else that could have been taken as aggressive, but his hand contacted Sheffield's face.

It was clearly intentional, and Sheffield was understandably pissed. Should he have pushed the fan at any time, no less before throwing the ball back in? No, but that's irrelevant. If the fans weren't allowed to sit there, this would have never happened, and that incident could have also easily gotten much worse. Maybe that's what it'll take!

It happened:

Regular season, 2019. Royals at Yankees. The Yankees are batting in the bottom of the 3rd with two runners on. Gleyber Torres rips one to deep left. The Gold Glover Alex Gordon goes back, back, he leaps, and…home run! For a moment, it looked like maybe the ball was off the wall, or Gordon's glove, or off the fan who reached out to grab it. Whatever happened, the umpire ruled it a dinger. Naturally, the Royals challenged the call.

It took a long time to review the play, and it was really, really hard to tell if Gordon would have made the catch. All we know is it certainly would have been a brilliant catch if he somehow came down with it.

Did the fan's hand pass the invisible line onto the field? The rule is clear: everything on the playing field belongs to the players, and everything on the fan's side of the fence can be shared. *The fans are allowed to interfere.*

After much deliberation, Gleyber Torres was ruled *out*! The Yankees had just increased their lead to 5-0, but now it was back to 2-0, and the runners were sent back to their respective bases. F-7 on your scorecard.

How many times does this have to happen? This time, we simply could not tell if the fan interfered or not as it is written in the rules. We have *no idea* what might have happened had there been no fan there. It may have been caught. It may have been a home run. As it was, that call could have gone either way, and that is unacceptable. The Yankees getting three runs or making their second out all rode on whether or not the umpires reviewing the call thought a fan interfered. A fan!

It happened:

I could go on and on and on, and that's the point. But Steve Bartman. Oh man. Game 6 of the 2003 National League Championship Series (NLCS). Marlins at Cubs. The Cubs lead the series 3-2 and are on the brink of making their first World Series since 1945. With the Marlins trailing 3-0 in the top of the 8th inning, Juan Pierre sends a foul fly ball down the left field line. Cubs leftfielder Moises Alou runs over for a look.. He leaps but can't make the play, as spectator Steve Bartman also tries to make the catch. Alou stomped around for a few seconds, yelling and disgustedly pointing up at the stands.

The ball looked like it may have landed right on that invisible line—very hard to tell if there was interference. It was ruled a foul ball, and then came the onslaught. The Cubs collapsed, and the Marlins put up eight runs. They won Game 6 and then eliminated the Cubs the next day.

One of the most famous plays in the history of baseball is grossly infamous because it involved a fan. Not to mention, Steve Bartman's whole life changed after that! His world was turned on its head as he became public enemy number one. Everyone scapegoated him. He was the most hated man in Chicago!

Meanwhile, the Marlins went on to win the World Series. To help Bartman cope with the trauma, Marlins owner Jeffrey Loria bought him a house in Florida.

Amazingly, Moises Alou admitted several years later that he wouldn't have been able to make the catch, no matter what Bartman did. Gee, better late than never, huh? Not this time. Had Alou spoken up right away, I still think Bartman would have taken *some* heat from the fans, but not enough to net him a house.

If the fans are not involved, it's a win-win for everybody. I know catching a foul ball or home run is cool, but that can't come at the expense of interfering with the players. Fans may not like being pushed back a few feet at first, but they'll understand. They'll realize it protects the players by upholding the integrity of the game, and it protects the fans by eliminating the possibility of being ostracized.

If the fans are allowed to continue to sit so close, then the rule needs to be this: any ball that goes beyond the fence, whether it's the outfield wall or the walls in foul territory, is now a home run or a foul ball. You must take away the chance of robbing home runs or making circus catches in the stands.

Obviously, no one wants that because everybody loves watching the fielders do everything they can to make a great play. But if you don't implement this rule, then the door to a home field advantage created by the fans remains open, and that's ridiculous. You could be sitting field level with your home team in the field. A foul ball can be hit your way, and you and everyone else can say on the behalf of your fielder, "Hey, get out of his way! Let him catch it!"

That's basically what happened in Game 6 of the 2019 ALCS between the Yankees and Astros in Houston. D.J. LeMahieu hit a two-run homer to tie the game in the top of the 9th. The ball barely cleared the fence, but the fans nearest the play gave their rightfielder, George Springer, the needed space to catch it. The craziest part is LeMahieu's ball was almost in the exact same spot José Altuve's non-home-run was the year before, when visitor Mookie Betts was interfered with.

SEPTEMBER CALLUPS AND THE 26 MAN ROSTER

I was very happy to hear that starting in 2020, September roster expansions must stop at 28 players instead of 40. But even with this change, baseball is still the only sport that ever expands its roster during the year. It's weird because you just played five months with 25 guys. It's crunch time, but now suddenly everybody is competing with and against a larger team?

With roster expansion, pivotal September games can be (and are) decided in extra innings by pinch runners, pinch hitters, or relief pitchers no one has heard of or will ever see again. A contender's season can either go down the tubes or be vaunted into October because of players who aren't allowed on a potential postseason roster. Limiting roster expansion to 28 players is a step in the right direction, but if you can't play in October, then you shouldn't be allowed to play in games that can determine who makes it to October.

I was also glad to hear the roster prior to September is expanding from 25 players to 26. These days, there's basically no bench anymore. It's all been replaced by a bunch of relief pitchers. It used to take a lot for there to be no one left on the bench. Now it happens routinely.

Once upon a time, your team had five starters, five relievers, eight starting position players, and seven guys off the bench. The idea of carrying a third catcher was not only plausible, it was also a pretty good idea. Suggest that in today's game, and you'll get laughed at because most benches only have four or five players on it. Then consider the fact that one of them is the backup catcher (whom the team generally avoids unless the starter gets hurt), and now your bench has dwindled to three or four. Throw in the fact that plenty of days someone will be unavailable because of a day-to-day injury, and now the bench is down to two or three.

It drives me nuts when you're in a game that's close and late, and there is no one to turn to in reserve. You're lucky if you can match up at all because you have so little selection between righties, lefties, guys with speed, and guys with power. By adding another player, you at least allow some flexibility to come back into play. Now wins and losses can be shaped a little more often by how shrewdly you use your backups, as opposed to just sending up whoever is left and praying.

Bill Madlock had a much different take on this. He was surprised the Players Association accepted both of these changes because he feels each change will limit players' earning potential. And because of this, he speculates a strike is coming sooner rather than later.

But that's only part of why Madlock expects a strike. So many future players could go to college, play two or three seasons in the minors, and not reach the majors until they're twenty-five. Being that they have to then put in six years of service before they can file for free agency, they might not be testing the free-agent market until they're thirty-one. A baseball player's prime years used to be expected during ages twenty-seven to thirty-three, but now that analytics says you're going downhill after thirty, this keeps these types of players from getting a real shot at free agency.

Like the front office, agents also use analytics to negotiate contracts. However, Madlock feels analytics costs players more money than it makes them because teams go through so many players now. Even though this means more players are making some money, team payroll still decreases because there are fewer players making big money. Madlock doesn't blame owners for trying to run a more cost-effective business, but the strike would be in an effort to shorten the amount of service needed to become a free agent. Instead of six years, maybe the Players Association can get it reduced to five.

THREE-HITTER MINIMUM FOR RELIEF PITCHERS

If there's anything that will make me stop watching baseball, it's this. It almost sounds like a Little League rule when you say out loud that relief pitchers must face at least three hitters unless he records the third out. I realize this rule's purpose is to save time, but Bill Madlock was once again surprised the Players Association agreed to this because of how directly it'll affect the outcome of a game.

I'm fine with saving time, but this is a bad idea. As much as I can't stand all the overmanaging and having relief pitchers take up half the 40-man roster, I'm not about to make anyone pitch to a certain number of hitters. The manager must be allowed to strategize. Joe Maddon also spoke against the rule, describing strategy as "sacred." Well, not only is the manager losing some of his sacred ability to manage but he's also losing it during the most critical parts of the game.

The rule will save time, but games are now going to be decided more because of rules and less because of strategy. It won't matter anymore who the best man is for each spot because it'll just come down to which relievers can adapt most adeptly to suboptimal conditions. We're going to see managers confusedly make a lot of really strange decisions because of the handcuffs they're being forced to wear.

This rule is also not going to save as much time as MLB thinks because of how much it favors the offense. More hitters will get on base because the manager can't always use an ideal pitching matchup.

I also think we will see a major reduction, if not a total disappearance, of the lefty specialist. Since the lefty specialist often only faces one hitter, it's hard to bring one in with fewer than two outs and tough righties to follow. Even if there are two outs, it's still risky.

The only thing I like about this rule is it'll be harder to be/stay a relief pitcher. Still, as much as I look forward to never seeing many scrub relievers ever again, it can't be for this reason. I hate a million and one things teams do with their bullpens, but I stand by their freedom to do it.

If MLB wants to save time, try skipping commercial breaks during pitching changes. Relievers don't need eight warmup pitchers on the mound because they just threw a bunch in the bullpen. Take four quick tosses, and game on.

RAIN-SHORTENED GAMES?

A baseball game becomes official once the losing team has batted five times. Seemingly, every season, at least one game goes fewer than nine innings because of rain. Some games are even called after five innings. What if the NFL called a game at halftime with a score of 14–6?

If a game is tied after five innings, it is suspended and completed at a later date. Why can't this be done regardless of the score? Maybe Major League Baseball is waiting for a team to miss the postseason by one game—a game which they lost 2–1 in five innings. Sooner or later, something like that will happen.

If the losing team has not batted five times before a game is rained out, the game is unofficial, and all stats are erased. Tie game or not, you have to start over from scratch. Once again, I fail to see why you can't just continue from where you left off.

SHOULD THERE BE AN ELECTRONIC STRIKE ZONE?

By his own admission, Bill Madlock yelled at umpires more than anybody he played with. In spite of that, he is still opposed to the electronic strike zone. He feels if the umpires miss a few calls a game, so be it.

Once analytics thoroughly showed us what the exact strike zone is (as it is defined in the rule book), we saw how inaccurate many umpire's strike zones were. The high strike was rarely called, and the corners were called too wide.

I started umpiring when I was a kid and stuck with it into my early twenties. I've umped two hundred to three hundred games, either behind the plate or in the field. It was mostly Little League baseball or softball, but there was some adult baseball and softball too. At all levels, everybody says they just want the ump to call a consistent strike zone. Fair enough. However, in my experience, most people haven't understood that calling a consistent strike zone is not so easy—especially when the pitching is all over the place, like it often is in Little League.

Since I have called balls and strikes for some highly competitive games, I can tell you that balls and strikes are often separated by centimeters. Sometimes a pitch that's barely a strike looks like a ball, and sometimes a pitch that's barely a ball looks like a strike.

Baseball has a ton of inherent variance, even if every call is correct. A pitch is a play, and there are hundreds of plays a game. If the plate ump gets 95 percent of the calls correct (which would be beyond outstanding), that means he still miffed fifteen calls in a game that had three hundred pitches. That's a lot! This time, I disagree with Madlock. I think there are enough incorrect calls per game to justify the electronic strike zone. I hate seeing hitters get incorrectly punched out in big spots as much as I hate seeing pitchers get incorrectly squeezed. One blown call can shift a whole game, and I'm willing to do what it takes to eliminate that.

As funny as it is to watch arguments over balls and strikes, I would gladly trade it for improved umpiring. Many umpires have huge egos, no matter what level they're umping (I certainly used to), and sometimes they call a strike to screw a hitter they dislike. The electronic strike zone will prevent that. Everyone will get along better, and the game will go faster, like MLB wants.

Even though I think the electronic strike zone will make things easier, I still relate to Madlock's viewpoint because I've gone back and forth about this many times. What if the new strike zone isn't flawless? What if the strike zone malfunctions and calls a ball on a pitch right down the middle or a strike on a pitch that was miles from the plate? What will we say then? It would get ugly. We accept human error as natural, but our responses to technological errors are generally much angrier. I don't think we could accept the electronic strike zone screwing up. We'd look at each other, wondering why we bothered playing when we're just at the mercy of whatever rules some computer decides to enforce.

There's nothing romantic about having the human error element directly change the outcome of games. If baseball were invented today, they would probably begin with an electronic strike zone. Either way, we might as well use it now. It's extremely radical, especially when you consider how aesthetically pleasing it is to watch an umpire call balls and strikes, but I think it's well worth the uncomfortable adaptation.

OVERTURNING TAG PLAYS

I love having video replay, but I've got an issue with the bang-bang tag play. We see challenges of a runner sliding into whatever base safely. He does everything right until he comes off the base by a fraction of an inch for a fraction of a second and then gets called out.

On one level, it makes sense to have this rule be black and white. If you're tagged off the base, you're out. Easy. Except now we're demanding a flawless slide from the runner in a way we never did because the naked eye can't spot such minor infractions. Maybe there should be some discretion. When the runner came off the base, did he *lose control* of the base with poor footing? If so, he's out. But if he did everything fluidly and still happened to come off the base for a microsecond, just let it go. This is tough because it creates a gray area, but it's worth a try.

VIDEO REPLAY IN GENERAL

Video replay is a must, but there are ways to improve its contribution.

The managers supposedly have thirty seconds to decide if they want to challenge a call, but that rule often goes unenforced, and that alone is unacceptable. Enforced or not, I would just get rid of challenges altogether and review every close play. Remove the video room so players can't steal signs, and have another umpire sit up in the press level with a monitor. Whenever there's a close play, have him look at it. I would much rather that than continue to watch a manager stand on the top step of the dugout, holding his hand up, hemming and hawing, waiting to hear if his crew upstairs thinks he should challenge.

Assuming MLB isn't going to do this, they can at least make every play reviewable. Currently, all calls on the infield stand because they occurred in front of the umpire. I don't get this because the purpose of video replay is to eliminate blown calls—not to fix a few and keep a few.

RUNNING OVER THE CATCHER

There are lots of ways to feel pain playing baseball. Many of them are rather odd:

- Getting drilled in the body, head, or face by a speeding baseball.
- Fouling a ball off any number of body parts (Jermaine Dye fouled a ball off himself and broke his leg during the 2001 postseason).
- Charging into a padded wall at full speed trying to catch a fly ball.
- Diving into the stands attempting to catch a foul ball.
- Flipping over a very short fence running after a ball in foul territory.

Some people believe baseball would have never outlawed running over the catcher if it wasn't superstar Buster Posey who got seriously injured from a home-plate collision. I also wasn't a fan of this rule's implementation, and especially so suddenly.

When I umpired Little League baseball, we always reiterated during the ground rules that the catcher cannot block home plate without the ball. It's a good rule if it protects kids, but it's not so good if pros also must abide by it.

I don't want to see catchers get injured, but it is so lame seeing a runner who is a dead duck at home just pull up and let himself get tagged out. You can play baseball every day because it is not a full-contact sport. However, the play at the plate is one of the only times baseball can get really physical. In my opinion, the play at the plate is the most exciting play in sports. If the catcher doesn't want to stand in there and get run over, then he doesn't have to. Of course, his decision is not uncomplicated. If he chooses to protect himself when he could have potentially kept a key run off the board, then now he must deal with being called out for softness and selfishness.

The best way to go about invoking this rule would have been putting it to a vote—rounding up all of the catchers who played X number of games in the last X number of seasons and letting them decide anonymously.

THE TAKEOUT SLIDE AT SECOND BASE

I was at Dodger Stadium for Game 2 of the 2015 National League Division Series (NLDS) when Chase Utley broke Mets shortstop Ruben Tejada's fibula. After seeing the replay a million times, okay, I agree. A rolling block isn't a slide. I'm fine with the most vicious and aggressive takeout slide, so as long as it actually is a slide.

But leave it to Major League Baseball to overdo the assurance that nothing like that ever happens again. In one offseason, the rules went from too lenient to too anal, and now we don't get to see middle infielders try to maintain their concentration during a hard takeout slide.

The rule doesn't need to be this strict. Let the umpires use discretion when calling runners out for an illegal slide. Did the runner start his slide well before the base, or was he just throwing his body at the fielder? With video replay, determining that will not be difficult. You'll have some disagreements, but that's okay. What's not okay is overreacting to one freaky play. Athletes get hurt. It's to be expected. If the solution is "Play not to get hurt," then now you're making everything about safety. Safety is not to be minimized, but you have to give some leeway. So just let the players play and the umpires ump.

THE REGULAR SEASON AND POSTSEASON STRUCTURE

The 16 game NFL season never plays any series. Regular or postseason, it's always one and done on the schedule because football is too brutal to do any other way. To win the championship, you have to win four postseason games, which is 25 percent of the number of regular-season games played. Four of the 12 postseason teams receive a first-round bye, but I still count the bye as a victory. Your regular season excellence is just rewarded by not having to play the first-round game.

In both the NBA and NHL, the 82 game season also primarily consists of playing whatever team once and then playing someone else. Only in hockey is there occasionally a two-game series in which each team plays at home.

Come postseason, the winner must get through four best-of-seven series. That means every postseason series, they play their opponent up to seven times as many games as they normally would in the regular season. By the end, the champion wins 16 postseason games. Comparable to the NFL's 25 percent, that is about 20 percent of the games played in the regular season.

Then there's baseball: a 162-game season played mostly in three-game series. Sometimes the series are four games, and occasionally they're two. Since baseball has the most variance, you need to play many games to get a good reading on who is the best.

Baseball's postseason is structured both similarly and differently to the NBA and NHL. To win the World Series, the similarity is that you play one five-game series followed by two seven-game series.

The difference is that, unlike the NBA and NHL, baseball's postseason series are only a little longer than its regular season's. If the NBA and NHL structured their postseason like baseball, their postseason series would all be a best-two-out-of-three instead of a best-of-seven. That is far less revealing as to who is the best, and that is what baseball does.

Not counting the wildcard game as a postseason game, baseball's champ only needs to win eleven postseason contests. Compared to the NFL's 25 percent, and the NBA and NHL's 20 percent, this is a tiny 6.8 percent of the 162 regular-season games played.

There are other large differences between baseball's postseason and the other major sports. The NFL, NBA, and NHL's postseason schedules are pretty comparable to their regular-season structures, but MLB's is not. During the regular season, you routinely play six to seven days a week.

Sometimes you play for almost three weeks straight. However, during the postseason, you usually don't play more than two days in a row.

The sudden frequency in off days makes a huge difference in managing your bullpen and especially your starting pitchers. Your relievers get more rest, but more importantly, you can hide your fifth starter in the bullpen. Over the 162-game season, you probably had a small combination of pitchers start 30-33 games to fill out the fifth spot. But when it's the postseason, you can go to war with only four starting pitchers.

Until the 2019 postseason, starting pitchers made October relief appearances plenty of times. Usually, they were in decisive games. But in 2019, the Nationals started Patrick Corbin in Game 1 of the NLDS versus the Dodgers and then used him out of the bullpen in Games 3 and 5. Max Scherzer also pitched an inning in relief Game 2 and then started Game 4.

Corbin made another relief appearance in Game 2 of the NLCS before starting Game 4. In the World Series, Corbin pitched an inning in relief in Game 1, started Game 4, and then pitched three innings in relief in Game 7. You *never* see these strategies in April through September, yet in October, they help decide who wins it all. I want to see baseball's champion win the same way they got to the postseason. The only problem is in order to do that, you'd have to make some super radical changes:

After a regular season of about 120 to 125 games, the postseason would start in mid-August. Then you'd have to lengthen the Division Series to a best of 13, the League Championship Series to a best of 15, and the World Series to a best of 17. With this structure, the champion would win 24 postseason games, which, like the NHL and NBA, is about 20 percent of the 120 to 125 regular season games.

You'd also have to cut down on the off days to ensure you keep using a fifth starter. If you played a best of 13, the home field structure would work as 3-3-3-3-1. As indicated by the bold numbers, you play the first six games before the first off day and then play the next game six games before the second off day. As for the best of 15 and 17 series, you could use a home field structure of 4-4-3-3-1, and 4-4-4-4-1.

The season would be done by mid-October. Some big side benefits would be that many players will have a longer career because of the shorter season, and it's also less likely you'd have to play the World Series in cold weather.

This clearly will never happen. I'm just mapping out what a baseball season would look like if it was structured like the other major sports. With this format, the regular and postseason dynamics wouldn't change, and it would also drastically lower the postseason luck factor—we're always hearing what a crapshoot postseason baseball is.

Obviously, a far more realistic proposal would be going back to a 154-game season (like it was through 1960) and making the Division Series a best of seven. The five-game series is short. These teams knock themselves out from spring training through September, so the least that could be done is heighten the task of beating the best team in the postseason's opening round.

One thing I definitely wouldn't do is have seven teams from each league make the postseason and allow two of them to choose whom they play in the first round. That structure is very convoluted and almost seems devised to use analytics even more—because if a team is allowed to pick whom they play, their selection will obviously be made based on analytics.

DIVISIONS, LEAGUES, AND IMBALANCED SCHEDULING

It wasn't that long ago that the National League still had three divisions totaling 16 teams, and the American League had three divisions totaling 14 teams. Back when each league still only had two divisions, the Atlanta Braves and Cincinnati Reds played in the West, while the St. Louis Cardinals and Chicago Cubs played in the East. If you know absolutely nothing about American geography, look at a map and let me know if you'd have come up with those same arrangements.

Even if every team was in the appropriate division, I would still say get rid of divisions—now *they* are a crapshoot. Just have one large league of 30 teams. Have everyone play each other the same number of times, and let the top eight teams play it out in the postseason. Whoever has the best record plays the team with the number-eight record, and so on. I know this will never happen because of money, but this would be the fairest thing to do.

Divisions stink for many reasons. In 2019, the Royals and Tigers lost a combined 217 games out of the AL Central, while four out of the five teams in the NL East had at least a .500 record.

In 2015, the Pirates went a stellar 98–64 in the NL Central. The Cubs were right behind them with 97 wins, but they each looked up at the Cardinals, who won 100.

Meanwhile, the 2015 Mets won the NL East with only a 90–72 record, and *three* of their four division rivals went at least 20 games under .500! The Pirates were shut out in the wildcard game for the second straight season, as they ran into another starting pitcher on a historic run (Madison Bumgarner in 2014; Jake Arrieta in 2015), while the Mets made the postseason with no additional obstacles. How is that fair? Having some luck is inevitable, but this is too much. And these are just a few examples.

The imbalanced schedule of playing almost half your season against the four specific teams in your division makes it much harder to tell who the best team in the league is because each front office only has to be concerned with assembling a team that matches up with their division. What do the Diamondbacks care about six games with the Brewers when they've got 19 with the Dodgers? Every game counts, but the best team would reveal itself far more easily if there wasn't so much luck involved in which teams you needed to be better than.

THE WILDCARD GAME

I hate it.

I like that it punishes the wildcard teams by making them go through another hurdle to get to the real postseason, but I would still get rid of the current format because it makes no fundamental sense. You almost always play three- or four-game series throughout the season. But as a wildcard contender, your season boils down to a single game?

When the original wildcard format had only one wildcard team, occasionally the top two wildcard contenders finished with the same record. They battled it out in a one-game playoff that was not called the postseason. All statistics counted toward regular-season game 163. I was fine with this because what else could you do? It sucked, having your 162-game season come down to one game, but so be it. Except now they do it on purpose.

To put the one-game playoff in perspective, one baseball game makes up 0.62 percent of the season. In football, five minutes and fifty-six seconds of one quarter makes up 0.62 percent of the season. What if the NFL decided that tiebreakers are to be settled by a one-game playoff that was only 5:56 long?

I would just go back to the original wildcard format. I doubt that'll happen, so my final suggestion is this: let the two wildcard teams settle their season in a three-game series, best two out of three. There will be no off days, and the top wildcard team will host every game. The second wildcard gets no home games because they're lucky to be getting a shot. If they want to compete in the postseason, then let them win a road series against a team with a better record.

THE DESIGNATED HITTER

We hate seeing a pitcher's poor hitting end innings or derail rallies, and we especially hate seeing them get hurt while hitting or running the bases. They're pitchers, so why should they risk injury doing things they're really not being paid to do? Isn't it more exciting to watch a real hitter?

I've gone back and forth on this for years, but I still say *no* to the DH (although I would sooner use it in both leagues than keep it the way it is).

Firstly, the DH takes away some of the strategy that can come into play. If it's the 8th inning of a 0–0 game and your pitcher is leading off, should you pinch-hit for him?

Secondly, and more importantly, baseball is a total sport. It's not a question of it being more exciting to watch a position player hit instead of the pitcher. As an everyday game, baseball is about producing offensively and defensively. There are no separate units like football, so it shouldn't be that way for a specific baseball player. If you're a slick fielder who can't hit, that's a tradeoff to your overall value, and vice versa. Some pitchers work really hard on hitting and can hold their own at it. Others don't work too hard, and they cost themselves.

GROUND RULE DOUBLE DISCRETION

Suppose there's a fast runner on first base with a full count and two outs. He takes off for second on the ensuing pitch. There's a high and deep fly ball, and it falls in play before bouncing into the stands. The runner was practically around third base when the ball went out of play, but it doesn't matter because the ground rule double always sends him back to third.

Why aren't the umpires allowed to just give the runner home plate? Is it that outlandish to assume he would have scored? We see how fast these guys run, we see how long it takes to relay a ball in from the outfield, and we're already using video replay anyway! It's only so often someone gets hurt running the bases (and that usually happens running to first base), so why can't the umpires review the call? Or, at the very least, be allowed to come together, discuss, and make their own determination?

There are enough breaks in baseball. This area of luck should not exist, and it's hardly a rare occurrence. I hate seeing teams get screwed out of runs because of the ground rule double's automaticity. If you're not sure whether the guy could have scored, then keep him at third base. But when it's as extreme as him crossing the plate and *then* finding out it's a ground rule double, just let the run count!

It happened:

Game 5 of the Red Sox's epic comeback against the Yankees in the 2004 ALCS. It's the top of the 9th in Boston with a score of 4–4. Ruben Sierra is on first base with two outs. The switch-hitting slugger Tony Clark pulled a shot to deep right field. It bounced on the warning track and into the stands, so Sierra was sent back to third base. Miguel Cairo fouled out to end the threat, and the Red Sox won in extra innings.

Ruben Sierra was not a base clogger. He wasn't the fastest guy at that stage in his career, either. Nevertheless, had the ball not bounced into the stands, Sierra probably would have easily scored the go-ahead run in the 9th inning of an elimination game. But because of this black and white rule, the Yankees were automatically burned. There was no possibility of Sierra being awarded home plate no matter how fast he ran. What if that was your team? Do you want to watch seven months of baseball only to have your biggest run of the year be taken away because of dumb luck?

I realize giving the umpires some discretion for these calls could get a little dicey, but it's hard to make things flawless. What matters is that this would be an improvement. Umpires would undoubtedly make far fewer mistakes using their discretion here than there would be runs automatically kept off the board.

DON'T THROW FOUR PITCHES FOR AN INTENTIONAL WALK; JUST GO TO FIRST BASE

I understand why Major League Baseball wants to speed up games, but alleviating pitchers of responsibility when there are runners in scoring position (RISP) is not the time to do it.

Intentional walks only occur at critical junctures because whenever they're issued, there is always at least one RISP. Why MLB is looking to save time when a big spot is developing is beyond me, but the pitcher should have to throw the four balls. IBBs don't take that long, they don't happen every game, and we've seen what kind of surprises can pop up. Sometimes the pitcher misses the spot, and the ball gets put in play. Sometimes the catcher sets up for the IBB as a decoy and then jumps back in the box to catch the pitch for a strike. The most common surprise is the pitcher psyching himself out and overthrowing the catcher for a wild pitch, or at least forcing him to make an acrobatic save.

Issuing the IBB may seem too easy to bother doing, but because they only happen during tense moments, you cannot erase the possibility of a huge mistake just to occasionally speed up the game by one minute.

There's one final element to the intentional walk. As it's happening, the suspense is building for the on-deck hitter. He has one last minute to brace himself and get ready. Not anymore though. Now it's just voilà! The intentionally walked hitter magically winds up on first base. Plenty of fans probably get confused for a second because the pitch-less IBB happened so fast.

SAVES AND BLOWN SAVES

During the 2016 season, the Mets were hyping up Jeurys Familia because he saved 52 straight games—a club record. What they didn't tell you was that during the midway point of that streak, he blew a four run 9th inning lead against the Dodgers (and then wound up the winning pitcher, of course).

I don't care that a four run lead isn't a save situation. If you inherit that big of a lead and still give it back, you deserve a penalty. The whole point of tracking saves is to show reliability when handed a lead. Therefore, your name should not go into the record books for a streak of saving games when you coughed up a giant lead along the way. Does it make sense to potentially penalize an athlete in a spot he can't be rewarded? I guess not. After all, Familia didn't blow a save. But at the same time, it does make sense because what he did was worse! It's either penalize him, or have an implosion silently pass through the record books because the game was too lopsided, and that's just silly.

What's also silly is that if you inherit a bases loaded jam with no outs and a one run lead, you get charged with the blown save if the opposition ties the game. It doesn't matter that it wasn't your baserunner. If the tying run scores while you're on the mound, it's recorded as your fault.

I'm going to say that one more time so you can see how fair it is. You don't get penalized if you personally give away a four-run lead, but you do if someone else's baserunner scores in a one run game.

Instead of having saves, why not create a point system? If you protect a one-run lead, you get one point *for every out you record*. Using the same system, protecting a two-run lead gets two-thirds of a point, and a three-run lead gets one-third of a point. If you blow a lead, you lose as many points as earned runs charged to *your* ERA until the game is tied.

Familia should have lost four points that night. It doesn't matter he didn't stand to earn any save points because that's the penalty for having that bad of a game. Thanks to the current system, only his ERA took a hit. Big deal. Analytics doesn't even care that much about ERA. And since nothing else indicated what actually happened, Familia got to maintain his fictitious streak of reliably ending games.

WINS AND THE QUALITY START

Can we please get rid of the stat called "wins"? It's been proven beyond a doubt that wins no longer mean anything because they depend so heavily on luck. Felix Hernandez won the Cy Young Award in 2010 with only 13 wins, and Jacob deGrom won the award twice with 10 in 2018 and 11 in 2019.

If you pitched six innings and allowed three earned runs or fewer, it's written down as a "quality start." That means you can make 30 starts with a 4.50 ERA and have all of them be considered "quality." Well, a 4.50 ERA from your fifth starter is pretty solid. But besides him, it is not. The quality-start standard should either be seven innings while allowing three earned runs or fewer, or six innings while allowing two earned runs or fewer. When you give up three runs after six innings, it's not often that you're a massive favorite to win beyond that point. So where is the quality?

THE OFFICIAL SCORING IS VERY MISLEADING

Scenario 1:

A fly ball is hit out to the centerfielder. It looks to be a can of corn. Clank. It hits off his glove for an error.

Scenario 2:

A fly ball is hit out to the centerfielder. It looks to be a can of corn. Instead, he misjudges it completely, and it lands next to him without ever touching his body. That's a single on your scorecard.

Why are you only charged with an error if the ball touches you? Why are you unpenalized when your defense was so bad you couldn't even touch the ball?

How about when there's a miscommunication between two fielders and a routine pop-up falls in? That's not an error, either, but why? Why does the pitcher get charged with a hit when it was the fielders who screwed up? It's not rocket science for the official scorer to watch the replay and see who should have taken charge. We calculate launch angle, exit velocity, route efficiency, and a million other things, but we can't give somebody an error unless they touch the ball? Why? And why do mental errors also silently pass through the box score when mental errors are the most brutal types of errors you can commit? Any mistake that costs your team bases and/or outs is worthy of statistical notation.

I know this doesn't affect the game. I also know this only affects a player's statistics so much, and analytics only has limited use for traditional stats. But as a fan, it's irritating to see constant inaccuracies over such simple things. The official scoring is supposed to let you know what happened. But because of silent errors, you can read a box score and have no idea about what game-changing plays took place.

Hitters are also frequently credited with hits when an all-but-routine play is botched. Official scorers have been doing this for hometown fan favorites for decades, but it was tolerable because it didn't happen that often. Now it's just about automatic, no matter who the home team is. If a play is even remotely more challenging than it would be for a Little Leaguer, the hitter gets a hit. It's like the official scorer feels guilty or evil for pointing out that someone made a mistake. This side of baseball has gotten very soft.

Ever since I started watching baseball, hitters have been credited with sacrifice bunts even when their intentions were *clearly* to bunt for a hit. Whenever we see a sac bunt, the hitter almost always shows bunt so that the bunt is easier to execute. What a sac bunter never does is stand in the batter's box looking ready to hammer. He never suddenly runs his hands up the bat right as the pitch is coming and then hauls ass to first base after he drops it down. That only happens when he is bunting for a hit. And considering how often a sac bunter doesn't run hard to first base, it should be that much clearer to an official scorer what a hitter's intentions were.

6ᵀᴴ INNING:
HOT, COLD, CLUTCH, AND CHOKING

The most obtuse conclusion analytics thinkers have drawn is that getting hot or cold, coming through in the clutch, or choking have little to no meaning. They believe athletes are always trying their hardest, so no particular situation affects their performance. They believe sports are essentially about muscle memory, and all that happens is never affected by emotion.

I was blindsided and completely dumbfounded the first time I heard these ideas thrown around. I'd have asked Bill Madlock about it if I'd remembered to, but it makes sense that I forgot because it almost saddened me that anyone could actually believe something so preposterously insane.

I agree athletes are always trying, but I don't think most athletes care about every result equally, because who hasn't been taught about the supposed importance of outcomes? Who hasn't been taught to try and make yourself thought well of by others?

At the end of the day, celebrity athletes are ordinary people like you and me. Sometimes they want something, and sometimes the fear of not getting what they want adversely affects their output. The want could also elevate their output, but the bottom line is one's performance is affected whenever there is any concern for the outcome—whenever one is caught up in what the result supposedly "means."

Denying the existence of being hot, cold, or clutch or choking is denying the existence of human emotions. This you cannot do, because these four things stem from human emotions.

It's bad enough that the dismissal of these four things happened at all, but what's extra deflating about it is that it takes so much fun out of discussing sports. It's great talking about the hot and cold streaks players go on. It's great debating players of present and past, remembering who is or was the most reliable with the game on the line, and whom you didn't trust, no matter how great their numbers were.

HOT AND COLD

You are hot when good luck and skills feed off each other. You have a big game, so you gain confidence and start performing even better. You consistently do everything right and then start getting lucky on top of it.

You're normally a .300 hitter. You should be hitting .350 over a great 100 AB stretch. But thanks to a few breaks, you're hitting .380.

You normally win $100 an hour. You're playing poker well enough to be up $14,000 over a 100 hour stretch ($140 an hour). But thanks to a few breaks, you're up $19,000.

You are cold when bad luck and mistakes feed off each other. You slowly seep into a bad habit or two, and suddenly you're slumping. You begin to lose confidence and perform even worse. You fall completely out of sync, and then start getting unlucky on top of it.

You're normally a .300 hitter. You should be hitting .240 over a poor 50 AB stretch. But thanks to some bad luck, you're hitting .200.

Cold streaks are prone to snowballing more so than hot streaks because people, due to their teachings, tend to choose dissatisfaction over satisfaction. Failing is dissatisfactory, and the satisfaction of success often proves to be underwhelming—there is still an unfulfilled void. This cold spell might have aggravated you into having some extra bad ABs. If it did, maybe you're only hitting .180.

You normally win $100 an hour. You should only be winning $3,000 over a poorly played 100 hour stretch ($30 an hour). Thanks to some bad luck, you're down $1,500. If this frustrating run aggravated you into playing some hands extra poorly, maybe you're down $5,000.

Cold streaks in poker snowball harder than they do in sports. One slump won't get a veteran major leaguer cut, but many longtime, talented poker players have, at least once, built up a large bankroll over a long period of time and then lost it over a short period.

HOW A HOT STREAK BEGINS

Las Vegas is home to the major leagues of poker, and that's why I came here. I wanted to play as big as possible for as long as possible. I had to know just how high and fast I could ride this insane roller coaster that requires many loose screws in your head to tolerate. I have played, watched, and talked many hours of poker with a long list of great players for well over a decade. From these efforts, here are just a couple more things I have taken away:

Never, ever has a player told me—or even so much as hinted—that they're playing the best poker of their career during a prolonged losing streak. Never, ever have I witnessed anyone play their best poker when they weren't having a big night. I don't speak from experience, but I think it's a safe bet that this is how it is in sports too. Plenty of athletes and poker players still play great through average or below average circumstances, but success is the fast lane to quality play.

Many, if not all, of the most popular games and sports include some short-term luck. Luck often helps get someone hot or cold because it boosts or thwarts their confidence. A hitter is having a normal season until suddenly, out of nowhere, pitchers start making mistakes against him. They could be throwing hittable pitches to anybody, but they keep throwing them to him. The hitter isn't exactly doing anything to induce these mistakes. They're just coming his way, he's capitalizing, and before you know it, he's hot and is confidently hitting tough pitching too.

A hitter consistently getting more hittable pitches than he could reasonably expect is like a poker player consistently receiving more donations from suckers than he could reasonably expect. Weak players lose patience and literally give away their money every day. After however much time of steady losing, they get into a hand and frustratedly decide this is the one they're going to take their stand with. Since they didn't use any actual strategy, whoever happens to have them beat gets the money. That money can always go to anyone, but it keeps going to one particular player. This player isn't exactly doing anything to induce the sucker's mistakes. The donations just keep coming his way, he's capitalizing, and before you know it, he's hot and is confidently outplaying good players too.

HOW A COLD STREAK BEGINS

Handling adversity is the key to succeeding at anything—you can't have a peak without a valley—you can't have a hot streak without a cold streak. Since how competitors handle adversity reflects how strong they are mentally, they must take them in stride to be great. Every competitor knows this, but many still get affected because mastering the mental side of competing is just as hard as the physical. This is why the most difficult challenge in being a winning poker player is playing through losing streaks. If you can't, you have no shot because there is going to be tons of them.

Poker players can get cold from beating themselves up too much after a mistake or two, but this usually happens after incurring a sudden barrage of rotten luck. Upon being battered around for a bit, players either recklessly chase their losses, or passively fear monsters under the bed. When passive, they'll start second-guessing themselves, reversing what would have been correct decisions into incorrect ones. Once that happens too much, they'll start solemnly expecting themselves to push the worst button at the worst time.

When a hitter keeps hitting the ball on the nose but has nothing to show for it, it is comparable to a poker player who keeps wagering his money as a substantial favorite, and then losing.

When a hitter keeps facing pitchers who are constantly executing their pitches, it is *somewhat* comparable to a poker player whose consistent optimal decision is to fold, no matter how much money they've invested in the hand.

The last two scenarios can also spark cold streaks because each competitor is consistently failing due to uncontrollable circumstances that could not be overcome. Regardless of whether a competitor allows tough streaks of any length to affect their performance, they'll always come and go—and never for any reason. I randomly start and stop being dealt profitable situations, hitters randomly start and stop seeing quality pitches, and line drives or softly hit balls randomly start and stop finding holes. In poker, you just have to patiently let probability do its thing. If you stay mentally strong through enough play, you'll get a proper-enough result. If athletes maintain focus through their inevitable ups and downs, they, too, will get a proper-enough result.

Since analytics can't account for a ballplayer's mental strength and how he handles streaks, it won't know at which particular times he might be performing above or below his usual value. Intuition will, though. That doesn't make managing as easy as benching whoever is cold and playing whoever is hot. However, knowing who is locked in versus who is totally lost should affect a manager's decision from time to time. No one can predict when someone will start or stop slumping, but if a manager can assess why his players are doing how they are, he'll know when adjustments are necessary.

To say there's no hot or cold is like saying *people* (not just athletes) never live through their egos. It's not that nobody ever stops being egoless, but we've all seen players get hot and cold. Some get really hot and really cold! And oftentimes, the streak at least partially stems from the egoistic ecstasy of success or misery of failure. Entire teams can band together when things are going their way, the same way that they can implode when things are going downhill. This is why you need an intuitive manager/head coach who adeptly knows what's going on inside the locker room. Any leader that does this will weather the storm of all the team's bad luck and make the most of their good luck.

GUTSY

While managing the Yankees, Joe Girardi pinch-hit for *Alex Rodriguez* in the bottom of the 9th inning in Game 3 of the 2012 ALDS versus the Orioles. The series was tied 1–1, and the O's led the game 2–1. A-Rod, who was huge in the postseason the last time the Yanks won it all in 2009, was really struggling. He'd heavily struggled many times in October, and the fans were always hard on him. He was cold again, and Girardi knew it. He told A-Rod that he was scuffing and wanted to take a shot at the short right-field porch with the forty-year-old lefty Raúl Ibañez. He had only an OBP of .308, but Ibañez homered off the righty Jim Johnson to tie the game, and then he homered again in the 12th inning to give the Yankees a 3–2 win.

Prior steroid use or not, past his prime or not, thirty-seven years old or not, it was unbelievable that Girardi pinch hit for Alex Rodriguez. Regardless of the outcome, I give Girardi infinite credit because it's so easy to just leave in A-Rod and his star-studded reputation. But Girardi didn't care. He saw what was going on and had the guts to accept it. That doesn't mean you must remove a superstar whenever he's slumping; however, this was another example of why sometimes illogic is logical.

MATCHUPS

Analytics thinkers believe a .300 hitter who has batted .467 against a particular pitcher in, say, 45 ABs will eventually revert to the means. That over enough time, his batting average versus that pitcher will regress to .300.

It takes a large sample size for a hitter's statistics to settle where it should, but it takes far fewer ABs to figure out who feels comfortable against whom when it comes to one particular matchup. No matter how much proof analytics can present as to why a lopsided matchup isn't lopsided, it will never be as reliable as what the eyes of a baseball person can see. If a hitter has great lifetime numbers against a certain pitcher, maybe the best thing to do is ask the hitter about it. Are the hits just falling in, or do you genuinely feel good when facing that pitcher?

Some radical results are more random than others, but it's too absolute to expect every radical result to balance out because not every athlete is the same. As athletes' strengths and weaknesses widely vary, so, too, do the results.

Tony Gwynn was a masterful .338 career hitter. Even more masterfully, in 107 plate appearances against the masterful Greg Maddux, Gwynn hit .415 with zero strikeouts. This was not all luck. There was nothing preventing Maddux from turning the tide on Gwynn, but until he adjusts, if Gwynn owns him, he owns him. And it makes sense that it took a Hall of Fame legend like Gwynn to master another Hall of Fame legend like Maddux.

WHAT HAS HAPPENED TO BASEBALL?

Facing Jorge Sosa, former All-Star slugger Carlos Delgado homered in five consecutive at-bats. Was that also pure luck? Is it not at all conceivable that maybe, just *maybe*, Delgado saw the ball a little better coming out of Sosa's hand than he did with other pitchers? That maybe, just *maybe*, Delgado was able to time him more easily? For crying out loud, timing is everything for a hitter!

Since it's pretty hard to pull off what Delgado and Gwynn did against Sosa and Maddux, I concede that luck played a part. But surely Delgado and Gwynn got unlucky against plenty of pitchers they loved facing, so we can say Sosa and Maddux made up for that.

It's freaky, but rewards have a funny way of coming in bizarre streaks. It's no different than a poker player who's been losing for a while and then suddenly wins it all back in a couple of nights. And like with Delgado and Gwynn, sometimes you get hot against someone you match up well with. In poker, that's when your 4.000 slugging percentage or .415 batting average comes in because an implosion becomes much likelier when a player is losing all their money to the same opponent—the streak can get in their head. Maddux expressed his frustrations about Gwynn, so I wonder if Delgado was inside Sosa's head too. Surely, Sosa must have remembered Delgado. Surely, at some point, he thought, "Oh, it's the guy who always homers off me."

I wouldn't expect Delgado or Gwynn to continue to dominate Sosa and Maddux so extremely, but I would expect them to continue performing above their averages. Matchup advantages are natural for competition because there are so many different skills to excel at. There are poker players I know I do better than against the field, but they do well against me. And I know it's not luck because I can tell when my opponents feel unthreatened.

CONFIDENCE AND LACKING CONFIDENCE

Since hot and cold streaks regularly snowball from confidence or lack thereof, they teach you that you must believe in yourself to excel. They're not wrong. When I'm confidently playing poker, I regularly notice small things that make big differences. Without confidence, I either pass on those opportunities because I'm afraid to lose, or I don't realize the opportunity passed until later. It happens in baseball too. A hitter may step in the box feeling unsure of himself and then take a first-pitch meatball. Or he thinks a fastball is coming, but he second-guesses himself and then gets blown away by it, whereas when he's confident, he's hungrily ready for it and most likely hits it hard somewhere.

The problem with the confidence concept is the very idea of affirming to yourself that you are confident already shows there is fear lurking underneath. If you really have what confidence supposedly is, then why would you think to tell yourself?

Whichever side of confidence you're on is always temporary. Confidence is one extreme of the pendulum, and the other extreme is lacking it—feeling insecure. Confidence yields good results, but it still bounces you up and down. When you're confident, it's like you're building down toward losing it. When you're not confident, it's like you're building up toward getting it back. Whatever extreme you're on, something will eventually swing you to the other. It's a vicious back-and-forth cycle because all you're doing is remembering past results and turning them into future expectations. But there is no past and future, so as one gets caught up in the illusion, they find themselves confident or not.

An example of all this is…professional sports! Teams play better at home! We've certainly seen a million road upsets, teams who've played great on the road, and teams who've stunk at home. Countless times, we've seen teams get cocky or tight *because* they were at home. Being at home is no automatic victory, but in general, home teams prevail. As home field confidence helps, it naturally goes back and forth through the whole league because everyone plays an equal number of home games.

The confidence cycle can create a false sense of security or bleakness. I've seen it many times in poker. Recreational players have their night where they finally go on a rampant winning streak. But rather than continue doing what they were before the streak began, now they think they're invincible and start playing hands they shouldn't.

They also might do this when they're losing. Normally there are certain hands they wouldn't play, but now they are because they're flustered and think they're "due." Or maybe they're dealt a hand they would normally play, but now they don't for fear of their dry luck continuing. Beyond that, they might fear playing a hand against an opponent strictly because they've been on a hot streak, or they might intentionally play a bad hand against an opponent strictly because they've been on a cold streak.

I realize even more just how senseless this "thinking" is when I write it down, but this is what goes on. And none of it would be any different from a hot hitter who starts swinging at more pitches because he thinks he can hit everything overseas. Nor would it be any different from a cold hitter who becomes apprehensive at the plate because nothing is going right.

My poker thinking has also often been quite senseless. When things are going great, I play very often. The well has water, so I keep going back to it. I'm confident, and I have more faith in the process, even though the process hasn't changed. When I go on losing streaks, they take a while to get through because I lose confidence. I get dejected and demotivated to play. I have less faith in the process, even though the process hasn't changed. Things eventually turn around, of course, but I'd be much better off if I left behind the whole ping-pong of confidence and just settled in the *middle*. Here I would play crisper and more often.

When in the middle, you neither have nor lack confidence because you are present. A hitter in the middle won't care if he's 0 for his last 20 or 20 for his last 20, because all he's focused on is the current AB. A poker player in the middle won't care if he's up or down $10,000 this session or this month because of good or bad luck. The only thing he'll be focused on is how to play the current hand.

If every baseball player was never with or without confidence—if they were always in the middle—then analytics would be that much more useful. It would be closer to the be-all and end-all the analytics thinkers already believe it is.

The ups and downs of sports, poker, and everything else aren't going anywhere. But you don't have to ride the swings with them. Be in the middle—go beyond confidence, because you'll always perform at maximum effectiveness and consistency, even more so than when you're confident. Be in the middle so that your success doesn't depend on the high of confidence, which can go at any moment without warning. Be in the middle, and you'll have no problem embracing the tension of high-leverage situations because you won't feel any. You'll be aware of the situation, but you won't feel any tension. You'll just be solidly balanced and that much more reliable. And if you don't come through, you won't feel any different than if you did. Being in the middle is like the ultimate confidence. It appears as confidence, but it's greater than that. It's a centered state of being—a total, harmonistic acceptance of yourself that doesn't forget you are always enough as you are.

I'm sure we've all settled in the middle before—if never else, probably when doing something we really love. But unlike the confidence cycle, once we've entered the middle, we're not bound to exit it, or stay in it, because the middle is presence—and we're always present or choosing to be somewhere else.

You always know when you are or aren't confident, but when in the middle, you never know. Your *awareness* is total, but you won't know that you are in the middle. If at any time you do know, then, paradoxically, you have left the middle—you have returned to the confidence cycle.

Being in the middle means you simply *are*—you are present—you are intuitively going about your business with no egoistic involvement whatsoever. There is no overanxiety, no pumping yourself up; the confidence cycle has ceased.

CLUTCH AND CHOKING

These two concepts are cut from the same cloth as hot and cold. Clutch situations don't just occur with athletes. Any time a person knows there's a lot on the line, they are in a clutch situation. Heavy-duty responsibilities can overwhelm a person, so if clutch sounds completely imaginary, then I guess you've never felt even a fleeting moment of pressure.

Scenario A:

You have a 9:00 a.m. job interview. You get a late start because your dog peed all over your new couch, your eight-year-old son wet the bed again, and then your college-freshman daughter calls you up to tell you she's pregnant. You finally leave. You're darting in and out of rush-hour traffic, which is now extra thick. Your head is spinning, knowing that in less than a year, you're going to be a grandparent. You wonder if you'll be able to get the stains out of your new couch. You wonder if your son will ever stop peeing himself when he's asleep.

But you still have work to do, so you keep your wits about you. Nothing too reckless. You run yellow lights, change lanes, and turn assertively when safe. You do everything that's rationally helpful. You make it on time and interview as if nothing unusual had just happened. Did you get the job?

Maybe, but it doesn't matter. You remained conscious. You maintained focus under stressful circumstances. That's clutch.

Scenario B:

You have a 9:00 a.m. job interview. You get a late start because your dog peed all over your new couch, your eight-year-old son wet the bed again, and then your college-freshman daughter calls you up to tell you she's pregnant. You think about postponing the interview, but you fear that'll look bad. You finally leave. Highly stressed, your hands sweat as you honk your horn, attempting to weave through extra thick rush-hour traffic. You almost crash your car, but you get there on time. Only you're worried. What will happen if you don't get this job now that grandparenthood is on its way? Will your son ever stop pissing himself? And what about the couch?

You want to tell the interviewer what's on your mind, but you don't want to give the impression you're stressed. You try to proceed like normal, but you never settle in. You remain nervous and don't come across like you're ready for this responsibility. Did you get the job? Maybe. But it doesn't matter. You lost focus. That's choking. Your attention was distracted by the past events and the future outcome of the interview. It was not on the interview itself. This doesn't mean you're a loser or that you'll lose focus the next time you have to deal with something important, but it's today's occurrence.

Regardless of these silly hypotheticals, I'm pretty sure everybody has had something crazy happen to them right before dealing with an unrelated high-leverage situation. Whether it was because of confidence or because you were in the middle, if you stayed on point, then no matter what bad luck or lack of good luck you incurred, you were clutch. If you lost focus, you choked. Losing focus can happen for any old reason, and it doesn't take much for it to happen, because the ego's power goes hand in hand with its fragility. Losing focus doesn't necessarily mean you were shaking to death—only a slight loss in concentration is a loss of focus, and it can and often does make a huge difference.

Choking once doesn't mean you'll always be a choker, just as one maintenance of focus under pressure doesn't mean you'll always be clutch. The terms are often thrown around too loosely, but all it takes is time to really see who's got a knack for staying sharp versus who tends to spin out.

The phrase "staying within myself" gets so repetitive, but it's not for nothing we hear that all the time. Staying within yourself is proper effort. Once you start reaching for something because you feel like *you* have to save the day, you're already choking. The same thing goes once you start fearing what will be said if you don't get the job done.

There's no doubt you can get lucky or unlucky in a high-leverage situation. A player's apparent hot streak, cold streak, or stretch of delivering or not delivering in big spots can be coincidental. So I understand why analytics thinkers think all of these concepts are false. However, a bit of luck and coincidence doesn't negate them *entirely* because that is getting overly absolute with logic. Since there are only so many coincidences, this just adds that much more importance to watching the games.

CLUTCH AND CHOKER TRAITS

Analytics figures that hitting a three-run homer in the 1st inning to break a 0-0 tie is no different than hitting one to tie the game with two outs in the 9th inning. Since you're always trying to win, and three runs is three runs, then what's the difference? In some ways, there is no difference. Analytically, the 1st and 9th inning are equally important and of equal leverage, but the 9th inning still carries another type of weight because it's the *9th freakin'* *inning*. Unlike computers, people have egos. They care about outcomes. Wins Above Replacement (WAR) tells us plenty about how valuable somebody is, but it has no idea what "clutch" even means, never mind who is. So you have to watch.

The most vital thing to understand about being clutch and choking is they are not fully quantifiable stats. Analytics thinkers dismiss the clutch and streaky concepts because they are relatively illogical, but this doesn't make the concepts fake. You just have to identify their occurrences intuitively, and this you cannot do without watching.

Clutch players *feel* clutch. It's a trust. You feel *good* when it's up to them. They might not be an elite player ticketed for the Hall of Fame, but they consistently thrive in big spots. Nothing to do with trying any harder—clutch players just embrace the big moments for their shoulders. They want to get up with the bases loaded, and they want the ball hit to them when the game is on the line. Clutch *people* are reliable because they are always ready to take on the biggest responsibilities—they are always aware of what's pertinent. Chokers are unreliable because they can't handle responsibility. They get caught up in the fear of making mistakes and are always looking for excuses to justify their setbacks.

As a poker player, of course I'm trying just as hard to make the correct decision when someone bets $200 into me as when they bet $2,000. But don't think you're going to convince me they're the same thing just because I'm trying my hardest. If I make the perfect play in a $2,000 pot, maybe it's comparable to getting a late-inning hit with RISP. If I make the perfect play in a $400 pot, maybe it's comparable to hitting a leadoff double in the 4th inning.

Clutch players are savvy. If a pitcher can recognize a hitter who either seems down on himself from slumping or a little stiff because he's up in a big spot, he can more easily exploit him. All the same, a clutch pitcher will also recognize when he must be careful with a hitter who is on fire.

Chokers like to give up when they're sluggish, but a clutch player can grind it out. A closer comes in and doesn't have his grade-A stuff, but he battles through it with all the fire and fury of his grace and grit. He doesn't lose faith in himself just because his body won't do what his mind wants.

The idea of being clutch and choking *would* be made up if everyone was Zen, so therein lies the biggest error in denying clutch's existence. The clutch concept is capable of going away, but for now, analytics thinkers are trying to impose an egoless computerized concept onto ego driven human beings. If everyone was Zen and just played to play instead of to win, only then would *no one* be clutch or choke. No one would ever feel any pressure because no one would think the result means anything. Everyone would just always be in the middle.

Except that's not even close to what goes on. The result means a ton to a ton of people, and the fact that the computer does not know this doesn't excuse anyone to deny something that is so plainly undeniable. Analytics thinkers proceed as if everyone is always in the middle, but they can't seem to grasp that this is not the case.

TIMING

Clutch situations aren't just at the end of games. A computer could never tell you this, but when you watch a lot of games, you'll feel certain critical junctures that carry large momentum shifts. And they can occur at any time. Maybe a pitcher didn't get the call on a 3-2 pitch to end the 4th inning, and now the bases are loaded. Then he gives up a two-out single, and a 3-1 game just became 5-1. Hits like that can be real backbreakers, and it's moments like these where games get decided.

How often does a slugger blast off at a critical juncture? Does he patiently wait for a hittable pitch, or does he insist on being the hero, chasing everything remotely near the strike zone?

If you're a rabbit on the bases, can you get yourself in scoring position down a run in the 8th inning? Or do you get tense and mainly try to steal only during the first six innings?

I'm not minimizing early game production. Every run you score now is one you don't have to score later. However, the later innings are the now-or-never times. It's not like the first few innings, when you still know there's time to make up for mistakes or missed opportunities. Knowing that can take some pressure off in the beginning of a game, but that luxury is not available at the end. So, if you're only productive when there's lots of time left but can't deliver when there isn't, that's bad.

Every competitor screws up, but clutch players' mistakes tend to occur at *very* resolvable junctures. They're more likely to make an error with a big lead than with a small one, whereas the choker seems to *save* their mistakes for the worst possible times. They have no problem hitting a three-run homer or turning a double play when their team is ahead 9-0, but when the game is tight, so, too, are their skills. When an entire team is tight in a big game or series, it's a reflection of the manager.

Understanding the clutch concept should not be hard. When you're down 9-0, you're thoroughly aware that striking out with the bases loaded to end a 9-0 game won't be as deflating as ending a 9-8 game. When it's 9-8, you're thoroughly aware your AB could decide who wins and that it'll probably be written about in the newspaper the next day.

EXPECTATION

The guys who seem to get the most clutch praise are the blue-collar grinders and bench players. Less is expected of them, so perhaps they get too much credit when they deliver. The guys who get labeled chokers the most are the superstars since their lucrative contracts come with hefty expectations. If they're clutch, it's par. If they aren't, they're a bust. Perhaps they get too much criticism when they come up short. Either way, if an athlete can't brush off fans' fickleness and unreasonable demands, they're in trouble. Plenty of athletes either couldn't handle the big markets, or it took them a while to get used to it.

Carlos Beltrán (more on him later) was a great example of this. The five-tool player had an improbable postseason run with the Astros in 2004, hitting eight home runs in nine games. When he signed a seven-year deal with the Mets the ensuing offseason, naturally everyone assumed he would hit 1.001 with RISP. Well, he didn't because he never got too comfortable in 2005. Beltrán's defense was awesome, but he didn't get momentum-shifting hits (despite an .888 OPS with RISP), he didn't steal nearly as many bases, and he had a major power outage. He only hit 16 home runs, and his slugging percentage dropped 134 points. He also kept bunting for base hits with multiple runners on base. Most of those attempts occurred in April, but it had every Mets fan wondering why the number-three-hitting, $100 million man was voluntarily bunting. I don't think Beltrán was afraid to swing away, but he was probably trying too hard to be dynamic.

The next season Beltrán did everything right. He was phenomenal. His slugging percentage jumped 180 points, and he hit 41 home runs. More than anything else, he finally looked relaxed.

One of the turning points in Beltrán's tenure as a Met came in the first week of that 2006 season. After struggling for a few games at home, he started hearing the boo birds again. Then one night, he suddenly hit a big home run in the late innings. Now the fickle fans who had been wanting so badly to cheer for their centerfielder wanted a curtain call. An irritated Beltrán, who was generally very quiet, stayed seated in the dugout until the forty-seven-year-old veteran Julio Franco approached him. With great leadership, Franco coaxed Beltrán into obliging the fans. He didn't look too thrilled about it. But he did it, and then he went on a season-long tear.

We'll never know what would have happened if this didn't happen, but I think Franco's words at least gave Beltrán a jolt. Surely, he'd have turned the corner eventually, being that he was so talented, but who knows when? This story is important because if players can be uncomfortable just with the environment they're playing in, they can certainly feel it when they're in a big spot.

MARIANO RIVERA

In his 1,105 regular-season relief appearances, this Hall of Fame closer had a career ERA of 2.06 and a WHIP of 0.97, and gave up 63 home runs in 1,233.2 innings (roughly one home run allowed every 20 innings). In Rivera's 96 postseason appearances, he saved 42/46 games (91.3 percent), pitched 141 innings with a 0.70 ERA and a WHIP of 0.76, and allowed only two home runs.

Rivera's postseason dominance is supposed to be a coincidence and too small of a sample size to mean anything? There is no question Rivera's stats would have reverted to the means if he pitched another 1,092.2 postseason innings?

Don't tell me Rivera is an exception, because the exception is the rule. It doesn't matter that he was an outlier. If *clutch* can apply to him, it can apply to anybody. Watching Mariano Rivera was a different experience. He was totally egoless—never confident or without confidence. It wasn't that he tried harder in October. He was just a master of remaining in the middle. And just because the computer can't comprehend this concept doesn't mean my intuition has deceived me. Whenever Rivera entered, whether it was at home or on the road, everybody knew the game was all but finished.

It wasn't just that Rivera would almost always save the game. It was the effortless way he did it. He had so many *clean* saves without a speck of agita. Pop-ups, weak ground balls, jam shots, broken bats, and strikeouts. Three up, three down. Mo was totally in control. He hardly ever blinked. It was kind of unreal. It was like he was in a different dimension.

Mariano Rivera once had a three-pitch inning in the postseason (it was a 1-2-3 inning, in case that wasn't obvious). How many times do you think that's happened? Was that luck too? "Dominant" closers look like completely different pitchers every October. Their confidence shifts to the other side because of the big game pressure, and Mr. Lights Out, who hasn't blown a game in blah blah blah, is suddenly throwing batting practice. The analytics thinkers say, "Oh! What a coincidence! Oh! What rotten luck!" Sure.

To some analytics thinkers, Mariano Rivera was just a relief pitcher who gets way more credit than he should because of how little all relief pitchers actually pitch. I get it, but when the closer comes in, he's recognized as the last piece to the puzzle. Everyone always says winning or losing is a team effort, but the closer gets remembered as the goat whenever he blows the game. He also often feels the guiltiest because it looks like everyone did their job except him. It's illogical, but this reality is what it is among athletes in tons of big spots. So those who glide through handling heavy responsibilities should be given their clutch due. These people are not easy to find.

MORE EXAMPLES

Now let's talk about one of the biggest errors ever made in postseason history. No, not Bill Buckner. Try second baseman Jose Lind in Game 7 of the 1992 NLCS between the Pirates and the Braves.

The Pirates, who once trailed the series 3-1, took a 2-0 lead into the bottom of the 9th inning in Atlanta. Terry Pendleton led off with a double, and then the lefty cleanup hitter David Justice followed with a ground ball to second base. It was hit hard but still a routine play. Jose Lind took three small steps to his right and went for the backhand, but the ball clanked off his glove for an E-4. He'd only made six errors that season. Ironically, this was also the lone year the slick-fielding Lind, who was primarily in the lineup for his defense, won the Gold Glove. So, instead of a runner on third base with one out, now the tying runs are on with nobody out.

Fast-forward. The bases are loaded, there are two outs, and the score is 2-1. The light-hitting backup Francisco Cabrera, who'd only had 11 plate appearances all season, delivered an earth-shattering pinch-hit two-run single to send the Braves to the World Series.

After booting Justice's ground ball, Jose Lind looked nauseated, like he knew he just choked. Did he? I don't know. If he didn't, then that error was some heap of hard luck for the Pirates—that their nearly flawless glove man suddenly did that in the 9th inning of a tight Game 7.

For the Mets, Daniel Murphy also committed one of the biggest postseason errors at second base in the 2015 World Series. In Game 4, the Mets were inching closer to tying the series at 2-2. With one out in the top of the 8th, and runners on first and second, with the Mets leading the game 3-2, Eric Hosmer hit a slow ground ball to Murphy. He charged hard, but it scooted under his glove. The tying run scored, the go-ahead run went to third base, and then everything fell apart.

After hearing his postgame interview following the Game 4 loss, intuition told me Murphy didn't choke. Only that Daniel Murphy did what Daniel Murphy had always been cited for doing, and that is harm you defensively a little too frequently. Now just because Murphy is not a slick fielder doesn't mean he couldn't have choked. I just don't think he did.

WHAT HAS HAPPENED TO BASEBALL?

In Clayton Kershaw's 2019 postgame interview after the Nationals beat the Dodgers in the NLDS, he practically admitted he's been choking all these years because he said that everything people say about him is true when it comes to October. It was visible and tangible how much his numerous subpar October performances have been weighing on him! I don't think Kershaw has buckled in big spots just because of that interview or what his postseason numbers are, so analytics thinkers can show as many stats as they want. It's not going to change what I and many others have known for years—that Clayton Kershaw has not looked like himself in October.

Barry Bonds's first five postseason appearances were in 1990, 1991, 1992, 1997, and 2000. From '90 through '92, he played in 20 postseason games, all of which were with the Pirates in the NLCS. He played in seven games in '97 and '00, all of which were with the Giants in the NLDS. Like he was for his entire career, Bonds was a superstar all five of those regular seasons.

October was a different story. In a combined 97 ABs and 116 PAs, Bonds batted .196, had an OBP of .319, and only hit one home run. He did, however, go 8/8 in stolen bases.

Bonds dominated October in his 92 postseason plate appearances in 2002 and 2003, but I don't think the differences in Bonds's physique and approach to playing baseball pre-and post-2001 need to be addressed.

Celebrity athletes with big egos are everywhere, and Barry Bonds was never too popular with opposing fans and the media because of his. Bonds took plenty of heat for his lackluster performances in October. And the more he struggled, the more he took. The situation compounded itself. Don't tell me receiving criticism for consistently doing nothing in the postseason meant nothing to him or the *many* other athletes cited for going backward in the big-time. Don't tell me it wasn't weighing on Bonds that he was known as a superstar well on his way to becoming an all-time Hall of Fame great, but also as a guy who couldn't do it in October.

It's not like I *care* that Barry Bonds and so many others have had their hard times in big spots. I'm just saying choking is real. And if choking is real, then clutch is, too, because you can't have one without the other. Some guys have a flair for the dramatic, and some guys don't. Some guys will be having a bad game or be in a prolonged slump, but when they finally break out, it comes at a critical time. Some guys will compile statistics and be a top player, but when playing for all the marbles, something just feels off. They're not the same. They're not flowing in their greatness like usual. They're *trying* to be great.

It isn't just random luck. This has been going on within anything that's competitive since competition began. Competitors step up or get overanxious *all the time*. We've been hearing them talk about pressing for decades. On any particular occasion, could it just be they made an error or got a big hit or threw a bad pitch for no special reason? Absolutely. Not every big moment was perpetuated by an athlete's internal feelings. However, since there have been so many big moments, you can't tell me all of them were luck. Plenty of them were mental. We don't always know which ones, but some are more tellable than others.

LOCATION

Since teams generally play poorer on the road, then a screaming crowd can definitely intimidate in a postseason game because it only takes the slightest shift in nerves to make a tense difference. Does Jose Lind field that ground ball if he's at home in Pittsburgh instead of Atlanta? Maybe. Does the twenty-two-year-old rightfielder Trent Grisham, who made zero errors in 42 games in 2019, cleanly pick up Juan Soto's base hit to keep the NL wildcard game tied 3–3 if it's in Milwaukee instead of Washington? Maybe.

Whether it's transitioning from the minor leagues to the majors, or from the regular season to the postseason, there's an adaptation whenever you change a competitor's environment. I've never played poker on TV. But if and when I do, the adjustment will be tuning out the hoopla and just continuing to do what got me on TV.

If a poker player is playing for bigger stakes than he normally plays, that, too, is a huge change of environment, regardless of whether it's on TV. As nerves pump from the thrill and danger of playing bigger, a commonly made mistake by a poker player raising the bar on himself is playing abnormally aggressively. They feel like they have to "do something" because now they're in a tougher arena. It's just pressing from inexperience. Athletes do it too. They're playing in big games down the stretch to make the postseason for the first time in their career, and the excitement causes them to at least be temporarily overanxious. They don't want to shy away from the moment, so they overcompensate. This is why we praise athletes (especially the young ones) when they look comfortable their first time on the big stage. They're so clutch, it's like they're even more relaxed for the big spot because they're finally playing for what they've prepared forever for.

7TH INNING STRETCH:
THE SHIFT

When baseball was invented, there was no scientific approach as to where every fielder should position themselves. It was, more or less, "You stand there, he'll stand there, and I'll stand here."

It seemed fine that way for decades, until analytics showed that repositioning your fielders can increase your chances of getting a particular hitter out. Of course, this wasn't a completely new concept. We'd seen shifts before, but they were rare and only put on against dead-pull lefties.

When the shift started becoming a regular thing, it expectedly began with the lefties. Crowding all the infielders on the right side of the infield and putting one in shallow right field looked a little stupid at first—all the hitter had to do was shorten up his swing and shoot a ground ball the other way or drop down a bunt. That happens occasionally. But shifting with the bases empty has proven to be very effective because it clearly takes away more hits than it gives.

Shifting with baserunners is another story. If all the infielders could competently know who is supposed to cover which base along with who is supposed to go after which ground balls, then fine. But that's not the case. We often see fielders looking at each other as routine ground balls roll past them into the outfield, and they frequently get confused about who is supposed to cover which base. It looks awful.

Infielders spend their whole baseball life learning where to position themselves, so it becomes second nature to know which balls are and aren't theirs. But now that a whole slew of shifts is constantly put on against righties and lefties in all baserunner scenarios, it's become very clear that fielders adapting to shifting is not going to be without some growing pains.

If teams are struggling to execute the shift with baserunners, they should at least consider that that using it might be more trouble than it's worth. Analytics might prove that shifting makes sense, but assuming no one will make a mistake is another loud example of why we shouldn't always default to analytics. As much as you must assess what the computer tells you to do, you must also assess how well you're executing its strategies.

8ᵀᴴ INNING:
WHEN DID PROFESSIONALISM BECOME UNIMPORTANT?

ILLEGAL SIGN-STEALING

A wise man who wishes to remain anonymous once said, "Baseball would be fine if it weren't stupid. But now it's stupid and there's cheating."

I've written this section under unprofessionalism, but don't get confused. The recent sign-stealing scandals are far beyond what it means to be unprofessional. I only put this part here because I didn't feel like putting it anywhere else.

My first question is, what was the Astros' Trash Can WAR? Since Houston is known for making especially good use of analytics, how much better was everybody's sabermetrics when they banged the trash can?

Mike Fiers has taken some criticism for snitching on the Astros after reaping the benefits, but I don't see how he was supposed to out his team *during* the season. Any Astro who was against Houston's illegal tactics was in a lose-lose situation. Regardless of what Fiers should have done or when he should have done it, I credit him for speaking up because we're always hearing about how honorable it is to not be a "rat." Well, the world would probably be much safer if it did have a few more rats because whistleblowing can protect people.

The worst part about this is thinking about how many pitchers there are in baseball (meaning most of them) who are fighting for their lives to stay in the big leagues. So many of them ask themselves every day what they can do to stay in the big leagues. Minor leaguers don't make much money, and plenty of them work multiple jobs in the offseason while they try to stay in shape. Imagine telling any of them they got bombed and sent down because the opposition knew what they were throwing.

It's unnerving that any of these ballplayers could treat their colleagues (even if they are their opponents) so disrespectfully. But I guess I shouldn't act so surprised. To many people, money is money, and winning is winning, no matter how either is attained.

The least heartfelt but most interesting things I heard were spoken by former manager Bobby Valentine in a radio interview in New York. Bobby V, who managed the Mets for about seven seasons, told Joe Benigno and Evan Roberts of WFAN that he thought everyone around baseball was at least aware that you *could* steal signs illegally. Whether or not they were is unknown, but Valentine also felt an owner should fire his manager and general manager if he ever found out they weren't either thinking about stealing signs or a way to combat other teams from doing it. I always loved Bobby V's rawness, so I expected no less than something like that from him.

Valentine also said if he knew his players were stealing signs, he, too, would have let it go on, like A. J. Hinch did. Valentine figures, shame on the opposition for letting his players get away with it. Ten or fifteen years ago, I'd have probably agreed with him, so I understand where he's coming from. I respect him for admitting that, as I don't think most people would have, but today, I strongly disagree.

I realize there are huge egos in sports with all the attention and money everybody makes. I realize there is bad blood out there and that there are certain teams, coaches, and managers other teams hatefully want to be beat. However, anyone who subscribes to the philosophy of or something like "If you're not cheating, then you're not trying!" will never feel an ounce of actual satisfaction on or off the field. No matter how much you "win," there is never any real satisfaction to be had when you have that little integrity—when you have zero integrity.

In learning how long illegal sign-stealing has been going on and also the extent to which it has gone, I feel disheartened and almost betrayed. I know the players didn't do this to screw fans, but as fans, we've been cheated out of our time. We've put all this effort into cheering baseball and its players, trusting that everything was real. Well, we were wrong because once again, everything is under suspicion. First it was the steroids, now this. At this point, the only good news is we can start over fresh and baseball will be clean from here on out. Maybe.

I didn't think anyone could beat the Houston Astros in 2017, 2018, or 2019 because they radiated a fearlessness I'd never sensed before. Something was extra great about them, and I couldn't figure out what it was. I knew analytics helped them build a great team, so I figured maybe that was it. But of course, fittingly, that was not the only reason. They were also cheating.

As flagrant as the steroid use was, I find stealing signs even more flagrant. You can be the biggest, strongest, fastest, and most athletic behemoth in the world, but it won't matter if you are easily fooled in the batter's box. If you don't hit in Major League Baseball, you don't play. It is that simple. You're either on the bench or gone.

Things change when you know what's coming, though. It doesn't matter at that point if you're a great hitter. If you know what pitch you're getting, your performance will elevate drastically. I don't think it's quite as lethal as knowing what your opponent's cards are when playing poker, but it's disturbingly close.

According to Rob Manfred's investigation, some Astros said they would rather not know what pitch is coming because it confusingly ends up doing more harm than good. Oh, sure. Don't get me wrong. I certainly see how it might be uncomfortable *at first*. The unfamiliarity of it all is grounds to make anyone overanxious and out of rhythm. But like anything else, you get better with repetition—*much better*.

After the Astros fired A. J. Hinch and the Red Sox did the same to Alex Cora, I really hoped the Mets would follow suit and get rid of Carlos Beltrán. As excited as I was by his hiring, it had to be done. I was not comfortable with a known cheater running the team because there was no upside to keeping him. He was going to be a distraction at best, and I imagine he was going to continue to steal signs because it just helped him win a World Series in his final year as a player. Holding onto Beltrán would make the Mets look too suspicious, which is why I'm surprised Major League Baseball didn't step in themselves and say he couldn't manage. I assume that was because the league decided not to punish players, but they could have made an exception for Beltrán since he was the only 2017 Astro getting set to manage.

I was surprised at how many Mets fans wanted Beltrán to stay on, thinking it wouldn't be a distraction. I suppose they thought this whole story wouldn't carry that long into the 2020 season, but I think it's going to carry on for *at least* the entire 2020 season. The Astros and Red Sox are going to have a sign on their back the whole year. That means the Mets also would have had they kept Beltrán. Besides, what did they need him so badly for anyway? He'd never managed a game! And if for absolutely no better reason, the Mets just signed relief pitcher Dellin Betances. He was on that 2017 Yankee team that got knocked out by Houston in the ALCS. Now he has to go play for one of the ringleaders that cheated his team out of a shot at the title?

It really doesn't matter what's written down since we all know what happened, but the Astros should lose every accomplishment by the players and the team since 2017, as should the Red Sox since 2018. Take away Mookie Betts's 2018 MVP, along with José Altuve's 2017 MVP. Let that prestigious award go to runner-up Aaron Judge for 2017 and Mike Trout for 2018. I don't care if there's proof of Altuve wearing a buzzer or not. Like Betts, his team cheated, so all rewards must come back. Fierce punishments should be enforced, regardless of whether that's what it takes to send the message, because it's fair to the rest of the league.

I would even take away Justin Verlander's 2019 Cy Young Award and give it to Charlie Morton. That seems ridiculous because the sign-stealing was used to help the Astros score runs, but I don't care. Who's to say knowing the offense was cheating didn't boost Verlander's output? I have no idea, but I am of the position that gives the Astros no benefit whatsoever. Just punish them completely. It won't happen, though, because there's no "proof" they cheated beyond 2017. We're supposed to believe they cheated their way to a tainted title in 2017 and then stopped. Okay. Cool story. I'm moving on now.

UNPROFESSIONALISM

These last few seasons, hitters of all ages and experience have been griping over every last borderline strike call. It's gotten so exhausting to watch because when you stack up one entitled complaint after another, each one just gets lamer than the last. They lose their meaning, and in turn the legit arguments also become less meaningful. It's like the boy who cried wolf.

There also used to be this unwritten rule that said you don't argue with umpires until you've been around the league for a while and have earned some respect. Whatever happened to that? Wherever it went, what's happening now is very improper. It's like a poker player having a baby after losing a big pot in which he had only a 51 to 58 percent chance of winning. I've seen that once or twice.

When Manny Machado was looking for a $300 million contract during the 2018 offseason, he said, "I'm not the type of player that's going to be Johnny Hustle."

I don't mean to single out Machado because it's irrelevant that he was the one who said this—do you think he's the only player who feels that way? That statement truly summarized modern day baseball in how excessively lazy it has gotten.

The downward spiral began off the field by overusing analytics, and now it's on the field more than ever. Laziness almost necessarily gets more leeway in baseball because of how much volume there is and how slow it moves, but it's never been this bad. Absolute laziness is so standardly accepted now superstars are proudly admitting they don't care about hustling. And don't tell me Machado is one bad apple or anything like that. This vomit is everywhere, and the overuse of analytics is part of why—not directly, indirectly. In a very natural way, the overfocus on analytics has led to teams overlooking the number one basic in being an athlete: *you hustle*.

The presumptuous inattentiveness that routinely goes on now has made everything lifelessly predictable. A pitcher gives up a single in the 6th inning. The managing staff assumes he's unraveling, so he is immediately replaced.

A hitter hits a fly ball. He assumes it's a home run, so he barely gets outside the batter's box, regardless of where the ball lands.

A sharply hit ground ball goes into the outfield. The jogging hitter assumes the sauntering outfielder will field it cleanly, and the outfielder assumes the hitter isn't running hard as he lobs in a lazy looping rainbow to complete the slow-motion play.

Bill Madlock agreed that today's baserunning is thoroughly atrocious. This, too, is an indirect responsibility of overdoing analytics because baseball is slacking on executing fundamentals. In the past few seasons, I have never seen so many players look so clueless on the basepaths. It's like they don't know what they're doing! And I'm not just noticing this now because the memories are more recent. I watched way more games as a kid, and it was never like this. There were baserunning blunders, but they were not constant or as inept.

Today's bunting is also pitiful. During the '90s, pitchers practically automatically got their sacrifice bunts down. A poor attempt would be if they didn't get it down until they had two strikes. Now most pitchers look like they've never bunted before. Their fundamentals are horrendous enough that this is probably another indirect impact of overusing analytics. Analytics doesn't like bunting—and for the most part, neither do I—but pitchers need to know how to bunt. Since they don't, I can only speculate that organizations are so concerned with grooming their pitchers to throw smoke that they've neglected teaching them anything about being in the batter's box.

With all the fundamental shortcomings we now see, there is simply no way upcoming ballplayers are taught the way they used to be. There is no way they are learning that much about every skill or professionalism because if they're not hustling, or bunting well, or properly running the bases at the highest level in the world, they probably never were. I'll say again to watch a game from today and then one from thirty years ago. You won't have to look closely to see and feel the differences because they're everywhere. It's stunning!

This really isn't about me being grumpy and too old school. Baseball just used to be played with a lot more heartfelt respect. It was great to watch because everybody looked like they cared. They literally were professionals. When a hitter got a base hit to the outfield, he made his opponent *work* by tearing out of the box *as soon as he made contact.* Then he'd make a hard turn around first base until the throw came in. It was beautiful! Nothing in athletics is better than good fundamentals.

It's as though players have forgotten that when you hit the ball, you run. Not take several slow steps to first base, watching like an inquisitive child and then choosing to run if the ball lands. How many times I've seen a replay of a guy hitting a triple and the announcer says, as the hitter is *rounding first base*, "This is where he turns it on!"

Why didn't he just turn it on after he dropped the bat? That would increase the chances of getting an inside-the-park home run, right? Isn't that good? No—apparently the object is taking your time for more than 25 percent of the bases; then you can start running. And, by the way, I want MLB to start referring to inside-the-park home runs as "quadruples."

The lollygagging and hotdogging has become so familiar, it's like no one sees how ugly it is. We'll see a hitter pop a home run that clears the fence by two feet, but all we see on the replay is his showy bat flip and celebration. Instead of the ball's trajectory, we see the hitter strut up the first base line. Am I the only one who still thinks the thrill of a home run is watching it go out of the ballpark? And not what kind of a spectacle the hitter can make of himself? Am I the only one who still likes watching a ballplayer put his head down and just go into his trot, no matter how far he thinks he's hit it?

Every few weeks there's another replay of some jackass hitting a deep fly ball who does cartwheels to first base and winds up settling for a *single* because showboating was more important than hustling. It goes on and on and on, and with no limit, because the aforementioned Manny Machado did this during Game 3 of the 2018 *World Series*. Baseball could not have looked any worse when that happened. But once again, it could have been anybody. In Game 6 of the 2019 World Series, superstar Alex Bregman carried his bat to first base after hitting a 1st inning home run and then handed it to the first base coach! Are you kidding me?

My dad told me this story from the Mets' 1969 championship season:

In the second half of the regular season, outfielder Cleon Jones relayed in a double hit down the left field line. Before another pitch was thrown, manager Gil Hodges personally walked out to left field. After talking to Jones and learning he wasn't injured, Hodges walked him off the field because he didn't hustle after the ball. I loved this story because Hodges had already made up his mind that Jones was coming out. The best part about this story was how much Jones admired Hodges for teaching him this lesson.

Hodges humiliating Jones in that exact manner is debatable, but the point is *all* players used to be held to a high standard of work ethic. It didn't matter how great they were. Cleon Jones was a Mets farmhand, a fan favorite, and a fine hitter. He had a career year in 1969, batting .340 with an OPS of .904.

Since vile tomfoolery like this is tolerated in today's game, I was elatedly blown away when Braves manager Brian Snitker pulled out superstar Ronald Acuña Jr. in the 3rd inning of a 2019 regular season game for being held to a single on a ball that hit off the wall. When I heard about it, I screamed, "Finally! *Finally!*"

Because that never happens. There's never a fine or any disciplinary action whatsoever to send the message that laziness is not okay. It just repeats and repeats while the announcers go on saying, "Well, he knows he should have been on second base there." Great.

WHAT HAS HAPPENED TO BASEBALL?

If you're still not convinced that unprofessional neglectfulness is widespread in baseball, then the slam-dunk proof is that Acuña pulled this exact same stunt not two months later—*in a postseason game.* In Game 1 of the NLDS versus the Cardinals, Acuña hit a shot the other way to right field and didn't even drop the bat! He just hopped, skipped, and danced around in the direction of first base until the ball hit off the wall for a single. The Braves were only holding a 3-1 lead in the 7th inning. They ended up losing 7-6, and then they lost the decisive Game 5 at home. Fitting, if you ask me.

A visibly *seething* Brian Snitker didn't pull Acuña out of Game 1. It was a no-win situation for the manager, but I agreed with his decision. I think Snitker was feeling damned if he does and damned if he doesn't, and ultimately decided that as appalling as Acuña antics once again were, this was not the time to reteach lessons.

Even with there being a second incident occurring in October, I still *almost* don't blame Acuña because this is what the twenty-one-year-old saw growing up—this is what he was permitted to do. No one demanded he hustle because analytics doesn't know what hustling is, and all everyone cares about is analytics. Today's teachers may not like the laziness, but they completely fail to recognize its relevance. It's like they've lost sight of the clear fact that the sign of a winning player—someone you want to play for your team and set examples for others—is someone who hustles!

I realize there are players out there who always hustle, and I'm sure there were lazy players fifty or a hundred years ago. But I don't care, because replacing hustle with an emphasis on fanfare is continuing to spread. Baseball's product is decreasing because fewer and fewer players care to play like they're supposed to—like they're paid to. This is not analytics' fault, but its indirect responsibility remains. The league is full of people who couldn't care less if you run to first base, and that kind of unprofessionalism is so uninspiring. You work all day, you come home, you're excited to watch a game, and you're greeted by somebody earning an eight- or nine-figure contract who takes a stroll to first base. Well, attendance is dropping, and the 2019 World Series received terrible ratings. Fans are getting turned off, and Bill Madlock agreed that the overuse of analytics has something to do with it.

I thought hustling was the point of playing sports because the whole idea behind competing is going hard. Hustling has always been my favorite part of competing because it's a privilege that my body can do what I want it to.

So when did it all go away? When did it become more important to just walk back to the dugout after you hit a pop-up on the infield? Justin Bour did that for the Angels in 2019. *In the beginning of the season* in April, he popped up and expected it to be caught in foul territory. With his bat still in hand, Bour turned his back, put his head down, and slowly walked away. Except the ball was very much in fair territory, about halfway between first and second base. The Mariners infielder wisely let it drop, and he turned it into an easy double play.

Like always, that easily could have been someone else because these abominations occur regularly. No matter how great analytics are, it's not what sports are about because no game can be properly played without sound effort and fundamentals. Imagine if everyone in the NBA started shooting with one hand.

It's not for nothing that baseball can be played six to seven days a week. It's mentally demanding, and you have to be in great shape to do it well for six months, but you don't do a ton day in and day out. You do, but you don't, because of how much time is spent watching and waiting for something to happen.

WHAT HAS HAPPENED TO BASEBALL?

Since baseball only requires so much hustle per game to begin with, when it is time to hustle, could everyone please just…hustle? And pick their battles with the umpires? And save their bat flips only for the epic game-changing home runs? The more bat flips we see, the less exciting they are.

I *accept* the occasional aggravated jog to first base when slumping. I accept conserving energy when the hot weather is sweltering with humidity during the dog days of August. I accept getting ejected after excessively arguing a bad call in a pivotal spot. I accept bat flips when they tie games or take the lead. I accept all of it! However, distinguishing frustration, conservation, and pure laziness from each other is not hard. Neither is showboating and genuine celebration. This is why my favorite poker players to play with are those who act like they've won before whenever they drag a big pot. They don't flaunt. They just carry on all the same as when lady luck smiles at the opposition. No conniptions, no berating the opponent, no whining at the dealer. They act like they've lost before.

The constant unprofessionalism that's been on display is making baseball very aesthetically displeasing. I know it's probably going to take a minute to undo this, but one place to begin this process is *toning things down* when it comes to analytics.

9TH INNING:
WHAT HAS HAPPENED TO BASEBALL?

Regarding the highly controversial interference call on Trea Turner at first base during Game 6 of the 2019 World Series, an annoyed Bill Madlock said maybe baseball should use the double first base for safety like Little League does. Let the fielder record outs by stepping on the left base (white) while the runner runs through the right base (orange).

I'm guessing you found most, if not all of what Bill Madlock said to be things any baseball fan could have said, and that's kind of the point: that it doesn't take a four-time batting champion to figure out that modern-day baseball is whacked out, that what is obvious to Madlock (and many former players, I'm sure) is just as obvious to fans because the hogwash is that glaring.

Pitchers like to say the best pitch in baseball is strike one. I don't know who coined that poetic gem, but I do know that analytics would say the best pitch in baseball is strike three. Gee, thanks.

WHAT HAS HAPPENED TO BASEBALL?

Taking analytics too seriously has left us with one very simple, very tragic result: baseball isn't as fun anymore. I realize professional baseball can't just be about fun because you have to optimize all of its elements, but all elements are not being optimized, and that's where the fun has gone. A bunch of people *think* the elements are being optimized, but that doesn't prove anything because we can all think ice is hot too.

At the end of the day, I am just another fan, and this book is just another opinion, but I've been playing poker for more than sixteen years. Whether or not you choose to agree is okay, but proper baseball and proper poker share more than just a few similarities—because what goes on in poker games and the skills needed to win at them are synonymous with many things. Baseball is just one of those things.

It was very cool when Game Theory Optimal became a tool for poker players. However, it was and still is difficult for many players to apply correctly, and people did and still do foolishly reject it if it doesn't bring instant results. Rejecting analytics isn't a problem for today's baseball thinkers and shot callers, but correctly applying analytics cannot possibly be any easier than correctly applying GTO because baseball and poker are both overrun with variables. Just as poker players shouldn't only use GTO, baseball people shouldn't only use analytics.

This whole "Just do what the computer says, and you can't fail" strategy is nothing more than a loafing fantasy. It is too good to be true because solving the universe of baseball and poker is not that elementary. Depending solely on analytics and GTO will bring success, but it's suboptimal for maximizing performance. To do that, you're going to need illogic to complement logic. Logic only exists because its buddy illogic is right there with it. If logic is not allowed to tandem with illogic, then illogic spawns itself because disallowing illogic is highly illogical. One way or another, illogic is going to be there so that logic can be too. You can either let illogic create itself intuitively, or you can force its existence by having an imbalanced overdependence on logic. Which would you like?

As poker continued to evolve and GTO became more and more developed, there was a little phase where people got carried away with it. It was nothing compared to the analytics epidemic, but for some time, there was a buzz going around that reading opponents was made up and that no one actually did it. Even though reading players had been around since poker began, suddenly it became a bunch of coincidental guesswork and was deemed unreliable compared to the foolproof GTO.

That buzz hasn't fully died down, but it's pretty dead because in poker, intuition reveals itself with an unrivaled straightforwardness. No other game seems so personal since you're playing for money, but it really couldn't be more impersonal. And impersonality always enables intuition to function because there's no ego.

This straightforwardness is why denying intuition and reads is as laughably dumb as thinking analytics is the lone way to win at baseball. It is as hardheaded as saying clutch play and pressure caused meltdowns are imagined. It's easy to say something is useless when you personally can't find any use for it, but other people might. And off the poker table, there are infinite situations to get reads on people or things. One place it can happen is a baseball field.

I am not denying the difficulty in reading people or situations on or off the poker table or baseball field because of how much people are trying to protect. Making keen reads is supremely difficult in the sense that the line between right and wrong is often very thin. Reads must be regularly correct; otherwise, they aren't worth it. There's some danger involved with illogic! You're really throwing yourself out into the unknown, but where does it say that's a bad idea?

The danger of illogic might appear more gaping, but this danger is no more mythical than believing logic is certain. Both approaches are uncertain. They are limited. And since there will never be certainty, let intuition guide you to an either logical or illogical approach in every situation because neither will ever be right or wrong. The only wrong you can do is to yourself by ignoring your intuition.

In a way, intuition is all that's ever really yours because intuition is unlimited. You are your intuition, so you, too, are unlimited. And when you follow intuition, you stop deciding—you only do. Formally overthought decisions end because you're simply yourself—imaginative—you go beyond thinking only about the intellect you've been taught. Your entire existence transforms into one continuous act of authentic spontaneity because everything you do comes from the inside, not the outside. There is no such thing as "extuition."

When I'm playing poker, most of the time I'm just sitting there. Folding, waiting, waiting, observing, and chilling in one spot like a lizard until an exploitative opportunity suddenly presents itself. The role of a good baseball manager requires similar behavior. Observe, let things unfold, and take either action or inaction when matters begin to press. Most of the decisions will be uncomplicated, and often they'll be really uncomplicated because intuition simplifies things—its simplicity is why it's wise. Otherwise, things are just a complex mess, and who wants that? Intuition won't always "work out" a certain way, but intuition is not about results. It's only meant to be trusted. Expectantly depending on it nullifies its use the same way it has for analytics.

Analytics is still new to most people, and it'll be a while before it's accepted. I've accepted it, but I've also accepted that baseball is decaying. I realize the analytics discoverers couldn't be tied down by baseball's roots in order to learn what analytics could contribute, but they've gone too far—they've ripped up the roots entirely.

I'll say one last time to watch a game from thirty years ago because you'll see how different baseball felt—different as in *purer*, because the roots were still there. A thing's roots still remain part of the process, no matter how much you expand and improve it.

Former Phillies manager Gabe Kapler made a very important acknowledgment during the 2019 season. He said he prefers analytics but noticed it was upsetting his team at times. Rather than insisting on analytics, Kapler curbed his use because he accepted pissing off his team is unwise. It was a very mature and flexible adjustment on Kapler's part. But more importantly, that statement summed up how often analytics should be used: *sometimes*. On any given day, that could mean 1 percent, 100 percent, or somewhere in between. Any amount is fine as long as analytics, GTO, and all other forms of logic are told to stand down whenever intuition recommends something illogical.

For all the "trashing" I've done to analytics, it is nuts to realize how little about baseball we understood. We used to look at a few very general things and draw very specific conclusions. This approach had many holes and exposing that is what analytics is for—looking deeper.

For decades, no one really understood poker either. Everybody pretty much just shot from the hip. The big winners were the most disciplined, but they were also the most intuitive—these go hand in hand. But after making some spectacularly intellectual discoveries, poker players finally learned it wasn't all about reads because math also plays a colossal role.

GTO has been great for poker's development because it only took so much enjoyment from it and only for so long. As for Major League Baseball, things are still a little bumpy. Until the use of analytics is properly harnessed, the joy will continue to fade. It'll only take a few people getting their head screwed on straight to undo the nonsense. But if they ever do, baseball will reclaim its beauty.

www.ingramcontent.com/pod-product-compliance
Lightning Source LLC
LaVergne TN
LVHW011839060526
838200LV00054B/4099